Automated Multi-Camera Surveillance
Algorithms and Practice

T0138059

The International Series in Video Computing

Series Editor: Mubarak Shah, Ph.D
                   University of Central Florida
                   Orlando, Florida

Automated Multi-Camera Surveillance
Algorithms and Practice

Omar Javed
ObjectVideo Inc.
Reston, Virginia, USA

Mubarak Shah
University of Central Florida
Orlando, Florida, US

 Springer

Omar Javed
ObjectVideo Inc.
Reston, VA 20191, USA

Mubarak Shah
University of Central Florida
Orlando, FL 32816, USA

ISSN: 1571-5205
ISBN: 978-1-4419-4626-3   e-ISBN: 978-0-387-78881-4
DOI: 10.1007/978-0-387-78881-4

Printed on acid-free paper

springer.com

To Captain Michael Holloway, Orlando Police Department (retired), who introduced us to video surveillance and provided enthusiastic support.

Omar Javed & Mubarak Shah

To my late father Mahmud Javed, who was always there for me; to my mother Dure-Shahwar who taught me the meaning of unconditional love, and to my wife Laila, who constantly brings joy to my life.

Omar Javed

Contents

Chapter 1
AUTOMATED VIDEO SURVEILLANCE

1.1 Introduction

In recent years, the deployment of surveillance systems has captured the interest of both the research and industrial worlds . The aim of this effort is to increase security and safety in several application domains such as national security, home and bank safety, traffic monitoring and navigation, tourism, and military applications, etc. The video surveillance systems currently in use share one feature; a human operator must constantly monitor them. Their effectiveness and response is largely determined, not by the technological capabilities or placement of the cameras but by the vigilance of the person monitoring the camera system. The number of cameras, and the area under surveillance is limited by the number of personnel available. Even well trained people cannot maintain their attention span for extended periods of time. Furthermore, employing people to continuously monitor surveillance videos is quite expensive. Therefore, a common practice in commercial stores or banks is to record the videos on tapes and use them as forensic tools, i.e., after a crime, the recorded video is used to collect evidence. However it will be more advantageous to have systems that have continuous 24/7 active warning capabilities so that security officials are alerted during or even before the happening of a crime. Specially the areas of law enforcement, national defence and airport security have great use of online systems. The Defense Advanced Research Projects Agency (DARPA) jump started the research and development of automated surveillance systems through the Visual Surveillance and Monitoring (VSAM) program 1997-99 [43] and the Airborne Video Surveillance (AVS) program 1998-2002. Currently there is a major effort underway in the vision community to develop a fully automated tracking and surveillance system. DARPA has initiated two new surveillance related programs namely Video Verification of Identity (VIVID) and Combat Zones that See (CTS). Major companies such as IBM, Siemens, Lockheed Martin and Boeing have programs underway to develop surveillance systems. Moreover, start up companies focussing on the area of automated surveillance are cropping up monthly.

O. Javed, M. Shah, *Automated Multi-Camera Surveillance: Algorithms and Practice*,
DOI: 10.1007/978-0-387-78881-4_1, © Springer Science+Business Media, LLC 2008

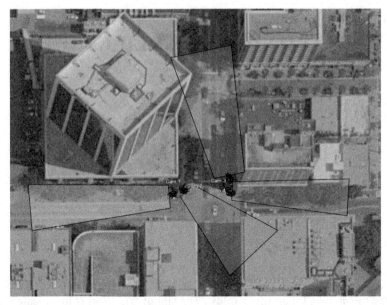

Fig. 1.1 An Overhead view of the Fields of View (FOV) of the cameras installed in Orlando Downtown for real world evaluation of our proposed algorithms.

1.2 Automated Systems for Video Surveillance

Automated video surveillance addresses monitoring of people and vehicles in real-time within a busy environment . A surveillance system must be able to detect and track objects moving in its field of view, classify these objects and detect some of their activities. It should also be capable of generating a description of the events happening within its field of view.

Existing automated surveillance systems can be classified into categories according to,

- the environment they are primarily designed to observe, i.e., indoor, outdoor or airborne.
- The number of sensors that the automated surveillance system can handle, i.e, single camera vs. multiple cameras.
- The mobility of sensor, i.e., stationary camera vs. mobile camera.

We are concerned with surveillance in an outdoor urban setting (see Figure 1.1) . In such cases, it is not possible for a single camera to observe the complete area of interest because sensor resolution is finite and structures in the scene limit the visible areas. Thus multiple cameras are required to observe large environments. Even then it is usually not possible to completely cover large areas with cameras, as is evident from Table 1.1 . The number of cameras required increases exponentially with the decrease in distance between the cameras (Figure 1.2). Therefore, there is a requirement for handling non-overlapping fields of view (FOV) of the cameras.

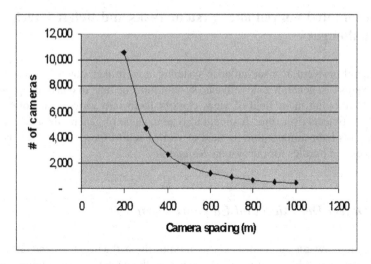

Fig. 1.2 Number of cameras to cover an environment vs. camera spacing. Source: DARPA Combat Zones that See (CTS) program [12].

In this book, we discuss and propose techniques for development of an automated multi-camera surveillance system for the outdoor environments. We also identify important issues that a system needs to cope with, in realistic surveillance scenarios. In summary, the purpose of a surveillance system is to record properties and trajectories of objects in a given area, and generate warnings or notify designated authority in case of occurrence of particular events. This level of interpretation is the goal of our research effort, with the intention of building systems that can deal with complexities of realistic scenarios.

Table 1.1 The number of cameras required for surveillance in cities. Source : DARPA's CTS program. [12].

Example City	Area km^2	Intersections	Overlapping Cameras	Cameras 100m apart	Cameras 500m apart	Cameras 1km apart	Roads km
Large	425	170,000	680,000	42,500	1,700	425	16,500
Medium	52	20,000	83,200	5,200	208	52	2,000
small	3	1,200	4,800	300	12	3	120

1.3 Automated Surveillance System Tasks and Related Technical Challenges

The general problem of a surveillance system can be broken down into a series of subproblems . In general, a surveillance system must be able to detect the presence of objects moving in its field of view, classify them into various categories, and track these objects over time. It should also be capable of generating a description of the events happening within its field of view. Each of these tasks poses its own challenges and hurdles for the system designers.

1.3.1 Object Detection and Categorization

The first step towards automated activity monitoring is the detection and classification of *interesting* objects in the field of view of the camera . The definition of an interesting object is context dependent, but for a general surveillance system, any independently moving object, e.g., a person, a vehicle or an animal, is deemed interesting. Detection and categorization of objects is a difficult problem because of the tremendous variety in object appearances and viewing conditions in practical scenarios. For example, the appearance of a person can vary considerably, depending on camera view, i.e., side view or top view. Furthermore, changes in lighting conditions and relative distance to cameras can also make an object appear different over time. What makes the problem of object detection and classification even more challenging in automated monitoring systems, is the requirement to perform this task in real time.

1.3.2 Tracking

Once the interesting objects have been detected, it is useful to have a record of their movement over time . Tracking can be defined as the problem of estimating the trajectory of an object as the object moves around a scene. Simply stated, we want to know where the object is in the image at each instant in time. If the objects are continuously observable and their shapes, sizes or motion do not vary over time, then tracking is not a hard problem. However, in realistic environments, like a busy street or a shopping mall, none of these assumptions hold true. Objects, especially people undergo a change in shape while moving. In addition, their motion is not constant.

Objects also undergo occlusion, i.e., the view of one object is blocked by another object or structure. Occlusion leads to discontinuity in the observation of objects, and is one of the major issues that a tracking algorithm needs to solve. Tracking objects under occlusion is difficult because accurate position and velocity of an

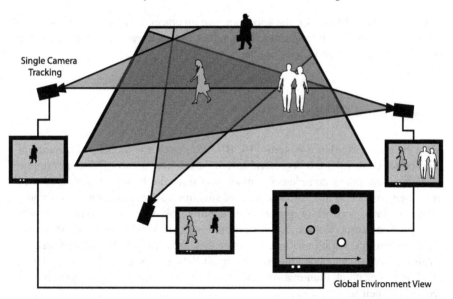

Fig. 1.3 A Distributed surveillance system. Inputs from each camera are integrated at the server level to determine a central view of the environment.

occluded object cannot be determined. In addition to the imperfection of input data, tracking methods also have to deal with imperfections in the output of detection methods. Detection methods are not perfect on their own and can miss the detection of interesting objects or to detect un-interesting objects. All these difficulties making tracking in realistic scenarios a hard problem for automated surveillance systems.

1.3.3 Tracking Across Cameras

In general, surveillance systems are required to observe large areas like airport perimeters, naval ports or shopping malls. In these scenarios, it is not possible for a single camera to observe the complete area of interest because sensor resolution is finite and structures in the scene limit the visible areas. Therefore, surveillance of wide areas requires a system with the ability to track objects while observing them through multiple cameras. The task of a multi-camera tracker is to establish correspondence between the observations across cameras, i.e., given a set of tracks in each camera, we want to find which of these tracks belong to the same object in the real world. An example of such a system is shown in Figure 1.3. Tracking across multiple cameras is difficult because the observations of an object are often widely separated in time and space when viewed from non-overlapping cameras. Therefore, simple location prediction schemes cannot be used to estimate the position of the object. Moreover, the appearance of an object in one camera view might be very different from its appearance in another camera view due to the differences in illumination, pose and camera properties.

1.3.4 General Challenges

Most existing surveillance systems [19, 101, 75] need a site model and camera calibration for deployment. It is preferable that the tracking approach does not require camera calibration or complete site modelling since the luxury of calibrated cameras or site models is not available in most situations. Also, maintaining calibration between a large network of sensors is a daunting task, since a slight change in the position of a sensor will require the calibration process to be repeated. Moreover, these systems are static in nature, i.e., once they are deployed they cannot adapt to changing environmental conditions, thus small changes in scene in terms of viewing conditions, i.e., quick illumination changes, or object traffic can have detrimental effect on the their performance.

In the next section, we give a brief introduction to the methods proposed for performing the surveillance system tasks and overcoming the challenging issues in this domain.

1.4 Introduction to the Proposed Video Understanding Algorithms for Surveillance

Figure 1.4 shows the information flow through our proposed multi-camera surveillance system, named *Knight*. This system uses a client-server architecture. A client computer is attached with each camera. The client is a self-contained single camera surveillance system named Knight . Each client contains an interest region detection module, object detection and classification module and a single camera tracking module.

The interest region module requires input of the raw image data. The output of the module is a binary image in which regions of interest are marked. The method for detection of these regions of interest consists of building a model of the background scene and measuring deviations from the model for each image in the video stream. This process, in general, is called background subtraction . Our proposed subtraction algorithm consists of three distinct levels, i.e., pixel level, region level and frame level. At the pixel level, unsupervised clustering of gradients and color features is employed to classify each pixel as belonging to background or foreground,i.e., the area of interest. At the region level, foreground pixels obtained from color based subtraction are grouped into regions and gradient based subtraction is then used to make inferences about the validity of these regions. Pixel based models are updated based on decisions made at the region level. The color and gradient models are

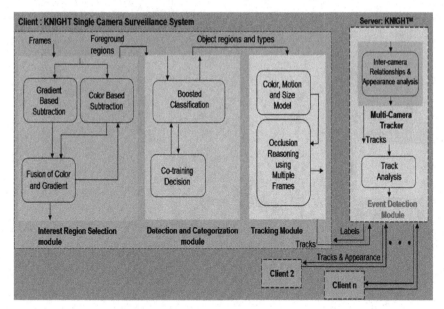

Fig. 1.4 Components of 'Knight' multiple camera surveillance system.

updated at each frame. Our method [58] adapts to changing illumination conditions and requires no manual interaction during initialization.

Once the regions of interest have been detected, they are forwarded to the object detection and classification module. This module consists of a boosted classifier for simultaneous detection and categorization of objects within the interest regions. The classifier is trainable online in a weakly supervised fashion, i.e., it requires a small number of initial labeled training samples and after deployment it automatically selects more samples for improved performance. The online selection of training samples is achieved by using the co-training framework. The basic idea is to train classifiers on two independent "views" (features) of the same data, using a relatively small number of examples. Then to use each classifier's prediction on the unlabeled examples to enlarge the training set of the other. In our approach, we use principal components of motion and appearance templates of objects as independent features. The major contribution of our detection approach [53] is that it is an *online* method, in which, if a subset of base classifiers selected through the boosting mechanism confidently predict the label of a data sample, then this data sample is added to the training set for online updating the rest of the base classifiers and boosting parameters.This online addition of training data significantly improves the detection and categorization performance of the system over time.

Once the objects have been detected and classified, they need to be tracked across frames. Tracking is performed for individual camera views first. At the single camera level, tracking is carried out as a region correspondence problem, given object

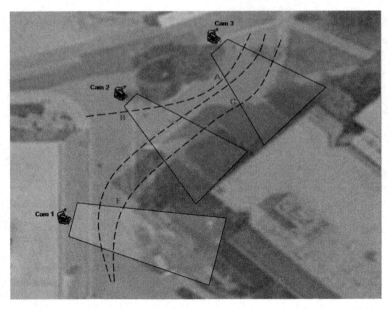

Fig. 1.5 Expected paths of people through the multi-camera system. These paths can be used to find relationships between the FOVs of the Cameras.

detection results. Location, shape and appearance similarity are used as cues for objects tracking [52, 56].

The results of single camera tracking are sent by the clients to a server over a network. These tracks, computed at individual cameras, are combined by the server to determine global track labels for objects. The method for cross camera tracking exploits the spatio-temporal relationships between camera FOVs [57]. These relationships are learned by observing objects moving across cameras in a training phase. The objects can take many paths across cameras (see Figure 1.5). However, due to physical and practical constraints some of the paths will be more likely to be used by people than others. Thus, the usual locations of exits and entrances between cameras, direction of movement and the average time taken to reach between cameras can be used to constrain correspondences. We refer to these cues as *space-time* cues. Parzen windows (also known as kernel density estimators) are used to estimate the inter-camera space-time relationships from training data, i.e., the probability of a person entering a certain camera at a certain time given the location, time and velocity of its exit from other cameras.

We also use the appearance of the objects to constrain the possible correspondences across multiple cameras [59]. Appearance of an object can be modelled by its color or brightness histograms, and it is a function of scene illumination, object geometry, object surface material properties (e.g., surface albedo) and the camera parameters. Thus, the color distribution of an object can be fairly different when viewed from two different cameras. One way to match appearances in different cameras is by finding a transformation that maps the appearance of an object in one camera image to its appearance in the other camera image. However, for a given pair of cameras, this transformation is not unique and also depends upon the scene illumination and camera parameters. We show that despite depending upon a large number of parameters, for a given pair of cameras, all such transformations lie in a low dimensional subspace. The proposed method learns this subspace of mappings for each pair of cameras from the training data by using probabilistic principal component analysis. Thus, given appearances in two different cameras, and the subspace of brightness transfer functions learned during the training phase, we can estimate the probability that the transformation between the appearances lies in the learned subspace. The correspondence probability, i.e., the probability that two observations originate from the same object, depends on both the space-time information and the appearance. Track labels across cameras are assigned by estimating the correspondences which maximize the posterior probabilities.

1.5 Book Organization

This book deals with the elementary problems of automated surveillance , i.e., object detection and classification, tracking in a single camera, and tracking across multiple cameras. In each chapter, we introduce the problem, report the current status of ongoing research, discuss the unsolved issues in that domain, propose a solution, state our results and discuss future work in that particular area. The issue of detecting and categorizing objects is described in Chapters 2 and 3. In Chapter 2, we discuss a method to detect interesting regions in images and, in Chapter 3, we describe the procedure for detection and categorization of objects in these regions of interest. Once interesting objects have been found they need to be tracked over time. Tracking in a single camera is explained in Chapter 4. A forest of cooperative cameras are required to perform surveillance over large areas. The details for tracking across multiple cameras are given in Chapter 5. We discuss the deployment of the system in real world situations in Chapter 6 and give concluding remarks in Chapter 7.

Chapter 2
IDENTIFYING REGIONS OF INTEREST IN IMAGE SEQUENCES

2.1 Introduction

The first step towards automated monitoring of activities is the detection of *interesting* regions in the field of view of the camera. In the context of a general surveillance system , any image region containing independently moving objects, e.g., a person,vehicle or an animal is considered interesting. The detection of such regions can be achieved by building a representation of the scene called a background model and then calculating the deviations from the model for each incoming frame. Any change in an image region with respect to the background model signifies the presence of an object or movement. The pixels constituting the regions undergoing change are classified as *foreground* pixels and are marked for further processing. The term *background subtraction* is used to denote this

process. The background models are usually built by using unsupervised learning mechanisms, e.g., EM (Expectation Maximization) [24], Parzen windows [27], etc. Modeling of backgrounds through unsupervised means is possible because it is assumed that almost all the video data that remains unchanged over time belongs to the background. The background subtraction process acts as a focus of attention method. Once regions of interest are determined, further processing for tracking and activity recognition ([5, 54]) is limited to these regions of the image. An example of the background subtraction output is shown in Figure 2.1.

In the next section we will discuss the major problems that arise in detecting interesting image regions using the background subtraction approach. We discuss the previous work in the field of background subtraction in Section 2.3. Our proposed solution to the background subtraction problem is discussed in Section 2.4. The results are given in Section 2.5. A discussion is given in Section 2.6.

O. Javed, M. Shah, *Automated Multi-Camera Surveillance: Algorithms and Practice,*   11
DOI: 10.1007/978-0-387-78881-4_2, © Springer Science+Business Media, LLC 2008

Fig. 2.1 Top row: Images from a camera watching a parking lot. Bottom Row: Corresponding output of the background subtraction module. White regions indicate areas of interest.

2.2 General Problems in Background Subtraction

The background subtraction methods, i.e., finding deviations from a scene representation, face several problems in accurately detecting regions containing moving objects in realistic environments. Here we briefly describe a complete list of these general problems.

1. Gradual Illumination Changes: In outdoor systems the illumination changes with the time of day. Change in illumination alters the appearance of the scene thus causing deviation from the background model. This may result in detection of foreground pixels even though an object may not be present in the scene.
2. Sudden illumination changes: Sudden illumination changes completely alter the color characteristics of the background, and thus increase the deviation of background pixels from the background model in color or intensity based subtraction. This results in a drastic increase in the number of falsely detected foreground regions and in the worst case, the whole image appears as foreground. An example is shown in the Figure 2.2.
3. Uninteresting movement: Sometimes "uninteresting" object also undergo motion, for example, flags waving or wind blowing through trees for short bursts of time. Reflection of moving objects from shiny or wet surfaces also causes problems. If a background subtraction method classifies such an object as a foreground region then a surveillance system might falsely conclude that an entity has entered within the field of view of the camera. An example of a spurious foreground region caused by swaying branches is given in Figure 2.3 column one.
4. Camouflage: If the object is very similar to the background then there will not be any signification deviation from the background model and therefore no regions

Fig. 2.2 Top row: Images from a scene undergoing an illumination change. Bottom Row: Corresponding output of the background subtraction module. The illumination change makes the image different from previous images, this change in brightness shows up as a region of interest.

of interest will be marked. An example of a camouflaged person is given in the Figure 2.3 column two.

5. Shadows. Objects cast shadows that might also be classified as foreground due to the illumination change in the shadow region. An example of a person casting a shadow is shown in Figure 2.3 column three.

6. Relocation of the background object: Relocation of a background object induces change in two different regions in the image, its newly acquired position and its previous position. While only the former should be identified as foreground region, any background subtraction system based on color variation detects both as foreground.

7. Initialization with moving objects: If moving objects are present during initialization then part of the background is occluded by moving objects, therefore accurate modeling of background in no longer possible. Many background subtraction algorithms require a scene with no moving objects during initialization. This puts serious limitations on systems to be used in high traffic areas.

A large number of background subtraction methods have been proposed in recent years which try to overcome some of the above mentioned issues. These methods are discussed in the next section.

2.3 Related Work

Background subtraction methods can be categorized on the basis of the features that are used to build the background models. The most commonly used feature is color. In addition, texture and edges have also been used to build background models. Another distinguishing characteristic for background subtraction methods is the background model being per-pixel or block based. Moreover, a variety of

Fig. 2.3 First Column: Images containing a tree swaying in the wind. Since the color patterns in the region containing the swaying branches are changing, this region shows up as foreground. Second Column: Notice the person at the top right of the image (highlighted by the green box). The person is wearing dark clothing in a dark region of the image. Since the color of person is very similar to the color of background, this person does not show up as foreground. Third Column: A person casting a shadow. Note that the shadow is fairly distinct as compared to the light background. The shadow area also shows up as foreground.

predictions techniques to estimate the current background have been used as well. Overall the background subtraction methods can be divided into three major categories, based on the type of features used for modeling the background. These are discussed below.

2.3.1 Background Subtraction using Color as a Feature

Most background methods used color as a feature for building the background model. Jain et al. [50] used a reference intensity image as a background model and performed simple intensity differencing between the current and reference images followed by thresholding. Therefore significant difference in intensity from the reference image was attributed to motion of objects. It was assumed that the reference image only contained a static scene. Olson and Brill [90] used a similar technique but used morphological operators to group disconnected regions. Azerbyjani et al. [128] replaced the reference image with a statistical model of the background. The color intensity at each pixel position was modelled by a single Gaussian distribution. For each incoming frame, the Mahalanobis distance between the color of the pixel and the corresponding Gaussian distribution was calculated. If the distance was greater than a threshold then the pixel belonged to the foreground (interesting) regions.

The above-mentioned algorithms suffered from the all the problems discussed in Section 2.2. Koller et al. [69] used a Kalman filter to update the background color model. This method was able to deal with slow illumination changes (Section 2.2). Stauffer and Grimson [115] extended the unimodal background subtraction approach by using an adaptive multi-modal subtraction method that modelled the pixel intensity as a mixture of Gaussians. In this algorithm, a pixel in the current frame is checked against the background model by comparing it with every Gaussian in the mixture model. In case a match is found, the parameters of the matched Gaussian are updated, otherwise a new Gaussian with the mean equal to the current pixel color and some initial variance is introduced into the mixture. Each pixel is classified as foreground or background depending on whether the matched distribution represents the background process. Gao et al. [35] compared the assumption of a single Gaussian versus a mixture of Gaussians to model the background color. They determined that the mixture of Gaussians approach is indeed a better representation of backgrounds even in static scenes. The model in Haritaoglu et al. [41] was a simplification of the Gaussian models, where the absolute maximum, minimum and largest consecutive difference values were used. This improved computation speed but made the model sensitive to outliers. Ricquebourg and Bouthemy [102] proposed tracking people by exploiting spatio-temporal slices. Their detection scheme involves the combined use of intensity, temporal differences between three successive images and of comparison of the current image to a background reference image which is reconstructed and updated online. Elgammal et al. [31] used Parzen windows to estimate the probability density function (pdf) of per-pixel color values, instead of assuming that each pixel has a Gaussian distribution. The advantage of this method was that it made no assumptions about the distribution of the pixel color values.

All of these methods, i.e. [115], [41] [102] and [31], could deal with slow changes in illumination, repeated motion from non-interesting objects and long term scene changes. Oliver et al. [89] used an eigenspace model for background subtraction. This model was formed by taking N sample images and computing the mean background image and its covariance matrix. The covariance matrix was diagnolized via eigenvalue decomposition. In order to reduce the dimensionality, only a fixed number of eigenvectors (eigen backgrounds) were used to form a principal component feature vector. To perform background subtraction, each image was projected on the the space expanded by the eigenvectors. Next the Euclidean distance was computed between the input image and the projected image. Thresholding this distance gave the interesting regions in the image. This method could deal with both slow and quick illumination changes in addition to repeated motion from background clutter.

Ohta [88] defined a test statistic for background subtraction using the ratio of color intensities. Toyama et al. [121] proposed a three tiered algorithm to deal with the background subtraction problem. The algorithm uses only color information at the pixel level. The region level deals with the background object relocation problem. Global illumination changes were handled at the frame level. This algorithm was able to handle sudden changes in illumination only if the model describing the scene after the illumination changes is known a priori. Harville [42] presented a multi-tiered background subtraction framework to update the mixture of Gaussians at each pixel based on feedback from other modules, for example tracking module, in a surveillance system. This method was also able to deal with both quick and slow illumination changes. However, the accuracy of background subtraction was dependent on the higher-level module.

2.3.2 Background Subtraction using Multiple Features

Recently subtraction methods have been proposed which use multiple features to build background models. The motivation is to incorporate information in the model that cannot be directly obtained from color. Horprasert et al. [46] used brightness distortion and color distortion measures to develop an algorithm invariant to illumination changes. Greiffenhagen et al. [38] proposed the fusion of color and normalized color information to achieve shadow invariant change detection. One flaw in these algorithms is that they have a high false negative rate, since they assume that any change in the brightness of color can only be caused by a change in illumination in the scene.

Jabri et.al [49] used fusion of color and edge information for background subtraction. However the algorithm used a pixel based fusion measure, such that either a large change in color or edges will result in foreground regions. Therefore this method cannot deal with sudden changes in illumination.

Some background subtraction approaches take the advantage of the depth information, Ivanov et al. [48] use the disparity map, D, which is computed off-line by a calibrated pair of cameras, the primary camera p and the auxiliary camera a. During the object detection, the image I_p obtained by the primary camera is warped using the disparity map $I_w(x,y) = I_p(x + D_x, y + D_y)$. Then difference between the luminance values of the warped image I_w and the image I_a obtained by the auxiliary camera is computed (disparity verification): $I_D = |I_w - I_a|$. Pixels with high values in the difference image I_D are then labeled as the object pixels. Gordon et al. [37] use the color and the depth features together to detect the foreground regions. Both of the depth based subtraction approaches need static backgrounds for good results, and are relatively expensive in terms of computation.

Li and Leung [77] use the fusion of texture and color to perform background subtraction over blocks of 5x5 pixels. Since texture does not vary greatly with illumination changes, the method was illumination invariant. Matsuyama et al. [82] used block correlation from background model to determine foreground regions. The background model is represented by a median template over each block calculated over a learning period. For each incoming frame, a correlation measure is calculated between the current block and the background block. In case the correlation is low, the entire block is marked as foreground. One important drawback of block based approaches is that block size effects the resolution of the results. Therefore, the interesting regions can only be marked in a coarse manner.

2.3.3 Finite State Space Based Background Subtraction

The finite state space based subtraction methods represent the variations in pixel intensity of the image sequences as discrete states corresponding to events in the environment, for example a pixel might be in shadow state or object state. Hidden Markov Models (HMMs) are employed to model the pixel states and the transitions between states. Rittscher et al. [103] used a three state HMM to model the intensity of a pixel with three possible states namely, shadow, background and foreground. Temporal continuity on a pixel state was imposed by using HMM, i.e., if a pixel is detected as part of the shadow then it is expected to remain a part of the shadow for a period of time before transiting to be the part of the background. Stenger et al. [116] used topology free HMMs to learn sudden light on/off events.

The HMM based background subtraction algorithms assume that there is a small number of predefined states. Therefore they cannot adapt to unforseen scenarios. They also require extensive initial training. Recently, Monnet et al. [86], and Zhong and Sclaroff [133] used autoregressive moving average (ARMA) processes to model the background. These methods are able to deal with non-stationary background, e.g., water waves or escalators. The autoregressive processes model the current state of a pixel in terms of the weighted sum of its previous values and a white noise error. In the next section, we present the proposed background subtraction approach.

2.4 Proposed Approach for Background Subtraction

The first question that arises for developing a background subtraction algorithm is, which features should be used to develop the background model? Color is the obvious answer. The advantage of using color is that dense per-pixel deviations from the model can be calculated. However, there is one caveat, color is very sensitive to changes in illumination. Image gradients, on the other hand, are quasi-invariant to illumination changes. The drawback of using image gradients is that they provide sparse information, therefore a per-pixel background/foreground decision cannot be made. Note that color and gradient based models complement each other's strengths. Our aim is to build a background model with color and gradients as features such that it has the advantages of both but none of their drawbacks. To that end we present a hierarchical background subtraction method that uses the color and gradient cues to robustly detect objects in adverse conditions. This algorithm consists of three distinct levels, i.e., pixel level, region level and frame level. At the pixel level, statistical models of gradients and color are separately used to classify each pixel as belonging to background or foreground. In region level, foreground pixels obtained from the color based subtraction are grouped into regions and gradient based subtraction is then used to make inferences about the validity of these regions. Pixel based models are updated based on decisions made at the region level. Finally, frame level analysis is performed to detect global illumination changes. Our method provides the solution to several problems that are not addressed by most background subtraction algorithms such as quick illumination changes, initialization of background model with moving objects present in the scene and repositioning of static background objects.

2.4.1 Assumptions

Our only assumption for the background subtraction module is that the camera is stationary. There are no restrictions on the orientation of the camera. The algorithm does not require calibration of the camera. The algorithm does not assume stable illumination over time. The algorithm also does not require removal of moving objects from the scene for initialization.

2.4.2 Pixel Level Processing

At the pixel level, background modelling is done in terms of color and gradient features. The color and gradient background models are discussed in the following subsections.

2.4.2.1 Color based subtraction

We use a mixture of Gaussians method , slightly modified from the version presented by Stauffer and Grimson [115] to perform background subtraction in the color domain . In this method, a mixture of K Gaussian distributions adaptively models each pixel color. The pdf of the kth Gaussian at pixel location (i,j) at time t is given as

$$N(x_{i,j}^t|m_{i,j}^{t,k}, \Sigma_{i,j}^{t,k}) = \frac{1}{(2\pi)^{\frac{n}{2}}|\Sigma_{i,j}^{t,k}|^{\frac{1}{2}}} \exp -\frac{1}{2}(x_{i,j}^t - m_{i,j}^{t,k})^T (\Sigma_{i,j}^{t,k})^{-1}(x_{i,j}^t - m_{i,j}^{t,k}),$$

where $x_{i,j}^t$ is the color of pixel i,j, $m_{i,j}^{t,k}$ and $\Sigma_{i,j}^{t,k}$ are the mean vector and the covariance matrix of the kth Gaussian in the mixture at time t respectively. Each Gaussian has an associated weight $\omega_{i,j}^{t,k}$ (where $0 < \omega_{i,j}^{t,k} < 1$) in the mixture. The covariance matrix is assumed to be diagonal to reduce the computational cost, i.e., $\Sigma_{i,j}^{t,k} = diag((\sigma_{i,j}^{t,k,R})^2, (\sigma_{i,j}^{t,k,G})^2, (\sigma_{i,j}^{t,k,B})^2)$ where R,G and B represent the three color components.

A K-means approximation of the EM algorithm is used to update the mixture model. Each new pixel color value, $x_{i,j}^t$, is checked against the existing K Gaussian distributions, until the pixel matches a distribution. A match is defined if $x_{i,j}^t$ is within a Mahalanobis distance, D, from the distribution. If $x_{i,j}^t$ does not match any of the distributions, the lowest weight distribution is replaced with a distribution having

$x_{i,j}^t$ as its mean, a fixed value as initial variance and low prior weight. The model parameters, i.e., the weights,means and covariance matrices are updated using an exponential decay scheme with a learning factor.

In the original approach [115], the weights are sorted in decreasing order and the first B distributions are selected as belonging to the background, i.e., $B = \arg\min_b(\Sigma_{k=1}^b \omega > T')$. Note that if a higher order process changes the weight of one distribution, it could affect the selection of other distributions as belonging to the background. Since we use input from the region and global levels to update our background, we adopt a method in which changing the weight of one distribution doesn't affect the selection of other distributions into the background. This is achieved by having a threshold on individual distributions, rather than on their sum. Any distribution with the weight greater than a threshold, T_w, is incorporated in a set of distributions belonging to background. A connected component algorithm is applied to group all the color foreground pixels into regions. Morphological filtering is performed to remove noise.

2.4.2.2 Gradient based subtraction

We use $\Delta = [\Delta_m, \Delta_d]$ as a feature vector for gradient based background differencing, where Δ_m is the gradient magnitude, i.e., $\sqrt{f_x^2 + f_y^2}$ and Δ_d is the gradient direction, i.e., $tan^{-1}\frac{f_y}{f_x}$. The gradients are calculated from the gray level image. .

In order to model the gradient of background intensities, we need to compute the distribution of Δ. We achieve this by initially assuming that for a given pixel (i, j), the highest weighted Gaussian distribution, say the kth distribution, models the color background at time t. Let $x_{i,j}^t = [R, G, B]$ be the latest color value that matched the kth distribution at pixel location (i, j), then $g_{i,j}^t = \alpha R + \beta G + \gamma B$ will be its gray scale value. Since we assumed independence between color channels, $g_{i,j}^t$ will be distributed as

$$g_{i,j}^t \sim N(\mu_{i,j}^t, (\sigma_{i,j}^t)^2), \tag{2.1}$$

where

$$\mu_{i,j}^t = \alpha m_{i,j}^{t,k,R} + \beta m_{i,j}^{t,k,G} + \gamma m_{i,j}^{t,k,B},$$
$$(\sigma_{i,j}^t)^2 = \alpha^2 (\sigma_{i,j}^{t,k,R})^2 + \beta^2 (\sigma_{i,j}^{t,k,G})^2 + \gamma^2 (\sigma_{i,j}^{t,k,B})^2.$$

Let us define $f_x = g_{i+1,j}^t - g_{i,j}^t$ and $f_y = g_{i,j+1}^t - g_{i,j}^t$. Assuming that gray levels at each pixel location are independent from neighboring pixels, we observe that

$$f_x \sim N(\mu_{f_x}, (\sigma_{f_x})^2), \tag{2.2}$$
$$f_y \sim N(\mu_{f_y}, (\sigma_{f_y})^2). \tag{2.3}$$

where

$$\mu_{f_x} = \mu_{i+1,j}^t - \mu_{i,j}^t,$$
$$\mu_{f_y} = \mu_{i,j+1}^t - \mu_{i,j}^t,$$
$$(\sigma_{f_x})^2 = (\sigma_{i+1,j}^t)^2 + (\sigma_{i,j}^t)^2,$$
$$(\sigma_{f_y})^2 = (\sigma_{i,j+1}^t)^2 + (\sigma_{i,j}^t)^2.$$

Note that even if gray values are assumed to be independent from each other, f_x and f_y are not independent. The covariance is given by,

$$Cov(f_x, f_y) = Cov(g_{i+1,j}^t - g_{i,j}^t, g_{i,j+1}^t - g_{i,j}^t) = Cov(g_{i,j}^t, g_{i,j}^t) = (\sigma_{i,j}^{t,k})^2 \quad (2.4)$$

Knowing the distribution of f_x and f_y, and using standard distribution transformation methods [14], we determine the joint pdf of feature vector $[\Delta_m, \Delta_d]$:

$$f(\Delta_m, \Delta_d) = \frac{\Delta_m}{2\pi\sigma_{f_x}\sigma_{f_y}\sqrt{1-\rho^2}} \exp\left(-\frac{z}{2(1-\rho^2)}\right), \quad (2.5)$$

where

$$z = \left(\frac{\Delta_m \cos\Delta_d - \mu_{f_x}}{\sigma_{f_x}}\right)^2 - 2\rho\left(\frac{\Delta_m \cos\Delta_d - \mu_{f_x}}{\sigma_{f_x}}\right)\left(\frac{\Delta_m \sin\Delta_d - \mu_{f_y}}{\sigma_{f_y}}\right)$$
$$+ \left(\frac{\Delta_m \sin\Delta_d - \mu_{f_y}}{\sigma_{f_y}}\right)^2,$$

$$\rho = \frac{\sigma_{i,j}^2}{\sigma_{f_x}\sigma_{f_y}}.$$

Note that for zero means, unit variances and $\rho = 0$, the above distribution becomes a product of a uniform distribution and a Rayleigh distribution. All the parameters in the above distribution can be calculated from the means and variances of the color distributions.

For each incoming frame, gradient magnitude and direction values are computed. If for a certain gradient vector, the probability of being generated from the background gradient distribution is less than T_g, then pixel belongs to foreground, otherwise it belongs to the background. There is no need to explicitly update the parameters of the background gradient distribution since all the parameters can be computed from the updated color background parameters.

Now, if multiple color Gaussians belong to the background model, then we can generate gradient distributions for all possible combination of the neighboring background Gaussian distributions. A pixel will belong to the gradient background model if it belongs to any of these gradient distributions. See figure 2.4 for an example of background gradient subtracted image.

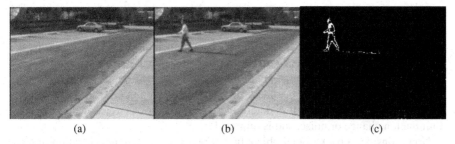

| (a) | (b) | (c) |

Fig. 2.4 Gradient based subtraction results, (a) first image in the sequence (b)150th image (c) gradient based subtraction. There is some noise but it can easily be removed by size based filtering.

2.4.3 Region Level Processing

The edge and color information obtained from pixel level is integrated at the region level. The basic idea is that any foreground region that corresponds to an actual object will have high values of gradient based background difference at its boundaries. The idea is explained in detail in the following paragraphs.

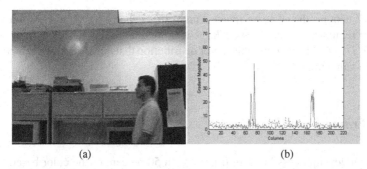

| (a) | (b) |

Fig. 2.5 (a) Image with a person and highlight (generated by a flash light). (b) Plot of gradient magnitudes at rows 60 (dashed) and 180 (solid). The plot shows that the person has high gradients at the boundaries. The highlight is diffused at the boundaries and therefore gradients are small.

Let I be the current frame and Δ be the gradient feature vector of its gray levels. Also, let $C(I)$ and $G(I)$ be the output of color based and gradient based subtraction, respectively. $C(I)$ and $G(I)$ are binary images such that $C(i,j) = 1$ iff the pixel at location (i,j) is classified as foreground by color based subtraction. Similarly $G(i,j) = 1$ if and only if the pixel at location (i,j) is classified as foreground by gradient based subtraction. Let $1 \leq a \leq k$ for the k regions in $C(I)$ that are detected as foreground. For any region R_a, such that R_a corresponds to some foreground object in the scene, there will be a high gradient at ∂R_a in the image I, where ∂R_a is the set of boundary pixels (i,j) of region R_a. Thus, it is reasonable to assume that Δ will have high deviation from the gradient background model at ∂R_a, i.e., $G(I)$ must have a high percentage of ON pixels in ∂R_a. However, if a region R_b

corresponds to a falsely detected foreground induced by local illumination changes, for example highlights, then there will be a smooth change in I at ∂R_b, (as shown in Figure 2.5). Thus the gradient of I at ∂R_b is not much different than the gradient of the background model, hence producing low percentage of ON pixels in $G(I)$. Following this reasoning, boundaries ∂R_a of each detected region R_a in $C(I)$ are determined. If p_B percent of boundary pixels also show up in $G(I)$ then the object is declared valid. Otherwise it is determined to be a spurious object caused by an illumination change or noise, and is removed.

Now, consider a background object that is repositioned to a new location in the scene thus inducing two regions say R_x and R_y in $C(I)$ corresponding to its newly acquired position and its previous position respectively. We want to classify R_x as a foreground region and R_y as a background region. Though R_x will usually have high percentage of boundary pixels that are ON in $G(I)$, the same is also true for R_y. This is due to the presence of edges in the background model at ∂R_y and the absence of edges in I at the same location. It follows that a foreground region R should not only have higher percentage of ON boundary pixels in $G(I)$ but these pixels should also lie on some edge of image I. Formally, we classify a region as a foreground region if

$$\frac{\sum_{(i,j)\in\partial R_a}(\nabla I(i,j)G(i,j))}{|\partial R_a|} \geq p_B. \tag{2.6}$$

where ∇I denotes the edges of image I and $|\partial R_a|$ denotes the number of boundary pixels of region R_a. Once a region R_a is identified as falsely detected, then for all pixels (i,j) in R_a, the weight of the color distribution that matched to $x^t_{i,j}$ is increased to have a value more than T_w.

2.4.4 Frame-Level Processing

The Frame level process kicks in if more than 50 percent of the color based background subtracted image becomes a part of the foreground. The Frame level processor then ignores the color based subtraction results. Thus only gradient information is used for subtraction. Connected components algorithm is applied to the gradient based subtraction results, i.e., $G(I)$. Only the bounding boxes belonging to the edge based results are considered as foreground regions. When the frame level model is active the region level processing is not done, since the color based subtraction is presumed to be completely unreliable at this point.

2.5 Results

The background subtraction method was tested on a variety of indoor and outdoor sequences. The sequences contained changes in lighting conditions, rain, windy

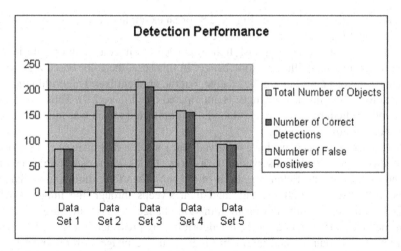

Fig. 2.6 Detection Performance over six hours of surveillance video.

conditions, different times of day, etc. The same thresholds were used for all the sequences. The values of important thresholds were $T_g = 10^{-3}$ and $p_B = .2$.

Please see Figure 2.6 to see detection rates of interest regions over six hours of videos in realistic scenarios.The performance was evaluated by manually determining the ground truth from six hours of videos at two different locations in Central Florida and comparing the ground truth to the results of the automated system. The data set was composed of five videos taken from different views and in different conditions, e.g., time of day, lighting, wind, camera focus etc. The accuracy of object detection was measured as the ratio of the number of correct detections and the total number of objects. 97.4% recall and 96.8% precision rates in detection were achieved.

In one particular sequence, there were moving persons in the scene during initialization. As long as there was overlap between uncovered background and moving object, both areas were shown as foreground. However, as soon as there was no overlap between the uncovered area and the moving objects, the region level process removed the uncovered areas (as shown in Figure 2.7) from the foreground since edges did not delineate their boundaries. Note that only color based subtraction would not have removed the uncovered regions as foreground, since the background color model learned at the time of initialization contained color values of the persons standing at that location. The boundary based gradient check might also fail if edges are present along the boundary of the uncovered region, however, the chances of this happening are obviously minute. The removal of regions based on gradient information is also useful in removing spurious foreground regions generated due to the motion of a previously static object. When such a object is moved, the uncovered region shows as foreground since the background model has no information about the appearance of this region. However, as edges do not delineate the boundary of the uncovered area, the region-level process removes the region from the foreground. Please see Figure 2.8 for an example of detection result when a static object is removed from the scene.

In another test sequence, a flash light was used to direct a beam of light in the scene to create a local illumination change. In this case, the color-based algorithm generated regions representing the change, but the gradient-based algorithm did not respond to the illumination change, as anticipated (see Figure 2.9). Thus, when the color and gradient results were combined the illuminated region was removed from the set of foreground regions.

In outdoor sequences, we have observed that a sudden illumination change over the complete area under observation is a rarity. Quick illumination changes are caused by movement of clouds in front of the sun. Therefore, illumination change starts from one area of the image and then sweeps through the image. Background subtraction results during illumination change, for both mixture of Gaussians method ([115]) and our proposed algorithm, are presented in Figure 2.10. The mixture of Gaussian method marks big regions in the image as foreground since the color in those regions has deviated from the background. However, since these newly illuminated regions do not have high gradients at the boundaries the proposed region-level processing is able to mark these regions as background and continuously update the color model by forcing the distribution of false objects into the background. Thus, only those areas of image in which illumination changed in consecutive frames show up as foreground in color based subtraction in the next frame. Note that, in Figure 2.10 second row, there are three people in the second image, two people close together on the top right corner and one on the left. The regions containing these people are correctly marked by the proposed method, while this is not case for subtraction through the mixture of Gaussian method (Figure 2.10 rows 3 and 4). Thus hierarchical processing results in greatly improving the interest region detection. More results are available on http://www.cs.ucf.edu/~ vision/projects/Knight/background.html.

2.6 Discussion

The two major contributions of the proposed work are:

- probabilistic modelling of per-pixel, gradient magnitude and direction based background.
- presentation of a novel method to combine color and gradient information in order to obtain dense, i.e., per pixel background subtraction results that are invariant to local illumination changes.

The proposed method gives accurate results in presence of both gradual and sudden illumination changes. It is also robust to the relocation of background objects,initialization with moving objects and moving trees and grass. Results on realistic scenarios are presented to demonstrate the viability of the proposed approach. One problem that the proposed approach does not solve is detecting camouflaged

(a) (b)

(c) (d)

Fig. 2.7 Initialization example (a) first image in the sequence (b) 30th image (c) color based results. Ghosts objects are visible on uncovered background. (d) Edge and color combined results. The ghost objects were removed because their boundary pixels did not contain significant edges.

objects. In this case, the camouflaged objects do not deviate significantly from the background model. One possible solution is to use both IR and EO sensors and employing R,G,B,IR information together as a feature vector for background subtraction.

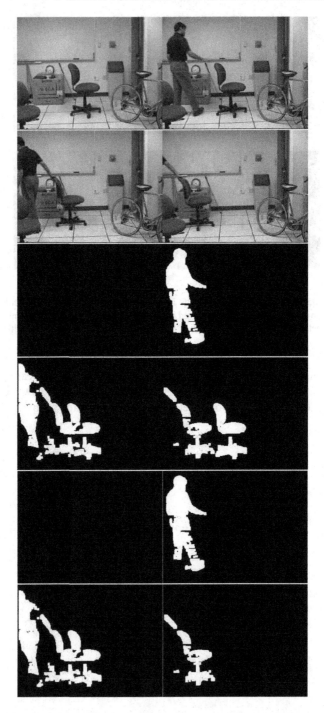

Fig. 2.8 Removal of a static (background) object from the scene. The first two rows show images at an interval of 30 frames from a sequence. The 3rd and the 4th row show the color based results using the mixture of Gaussians. The last two rows show the hierarchical background subtraction results. Note that the removal of object is successfully detected and the uncovered area does not show up as foreground region.

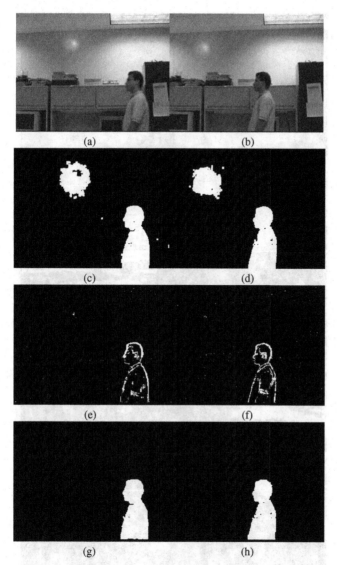

Fig. 2.9 (a)(b) Two frames from a sequence with a person and a highlight in the foreground. (c)(d) color background subtraction using Mixture of Gaussians. Note that Illumination change is causing spurious foreground regions. (e)(f) edge based background subtraction (g)(h) edge and color combined results.

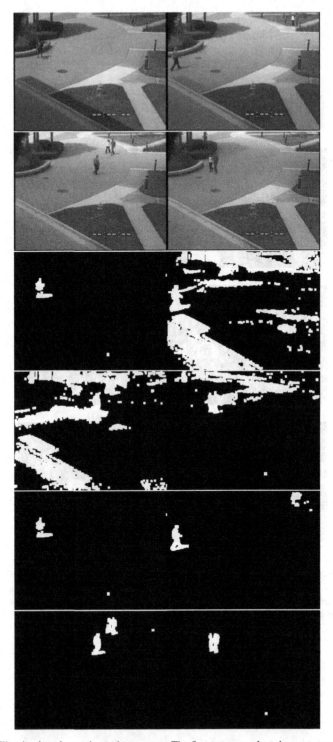

Fig. 2.10 Illumination change in outdoor scenes. The first two rows show images at an interval of 70 frames from a sequence. The 3rd and the 4th row show the color based results using the Mixture of Gaussians method with no feedback from higher level. The last two rows show the hierarchical background subtraction results. All the people have been successfully detected.

Chapter 3
OBJECT DETECTION AND CATEGORIZATION

3.1 Introduction

The detection of moving objects in a scene is of utmost importance for most tracking and video analysis systems. The background subtraction algorithm serves as a focus of attention method but provides no information about,

- the number of objects in a region of interest, and
- the type of object or objects in the region of interest.

In order to locate and classify the objects, we need specific information about the objects of interest. This assumes that only a limited number of well defined object types are relevant for surveillance. Fortunately, for most surveillance systems the objects of interest are usually people and vehicles. Supervised classification methods ([106, 94, 125]) have been successfully used for detection of such objects. These classification methods map feature vectors obtained from images to object labels. Such methods work in two distinct phases, namely training phase and testing phase. In the training phase, the classifiers are provided with labeled feature vectors, representing objects that need to be classified. The feature vectors used to represent objects can comprise of appearance, motion and shape information. The classification methods partition the feature space into the required object classes. During the test phase, the classifier take the input feature vector representing an image region and classifies it as an object category based on the feature space partitioning, learned in the training phase. There are some limitations of the supervised classification methods. These methods require extremely large number of labeled training examples to ensure good performance in the test phase. Moreover, the classifier parameters are fixed at the end of the training phase, and therefore the classifier can not cope with conditions during test phase that are not catered for in the training data. In this chapter, we propose a *co-training* based algorithm that does not have the aforemention limitations. The algorithm continuously labels incoming data and uses it for online update of the classifier that was initially trained from a small labeled example set.

In the next section, we discuss the challenges involved in solving the detection and categorization problem. In Section 3.3, we discuss the related work. In Section

O. Javed, M. Shah, *Automated Multi-Camera Surveillance: Algorithms and Practice*, DOI: 10.1007/978-0-387-78881-4_3, © Springer Science+Business Media, LLC 2008

3.4, we give the overview of our co-training based boosted classification framework. In Section 3.5, we discuss the issues of feature selection and modeling of base classifiers for boosting. In Section 3.6, we describe the co-training framework in the context of an online boosted classifier. In Section 3.7, we discuss ways to measure the effectiveness of co-training in improving classifiers. In Section 5.7, we present the results and give the concluding remarks in Section 3.9

3.2 Problems in Object Categorization

The general problems faced by any object categorization system in a realistic surveillance scenario are presented below.

- Large variation in object appearance: The appearance of a person can vary widely depending upon what he/she is wearing and also what he/she is doing. For example, the appearance of a walking person is very different from a person crawling on the ground. Vehicles also come in a large variety of shapes and sizes, making categorization difficult.
- Wide variety of viewing conditions: In many scenarios, classification has to be performed in cameras with different viewing angles and different camera parameters. Moreover, the illumination in the scene usually changes over time. All these variations can make consistently accurate classification difficult.

3.3 Related Work

The object categorization methods used in surveillance related scenarios can be divided into three major classes depending on the type of features and classifiers used for this purpose. The details for each class of methods are discussed in the following subsections.

3.3.1 Periodicity Based Categorization

These methods classify objects as periodically moving objects or non-periodic objects. The intuition behind such methods is that walking people undergo periodic motion while vehicles do not, thus periodicity detection can be used distinguish between the two.

Tsai et. al. [122] analyzed periodic motion of objects to perform motion based recognition. In this method, specific points on the objects were tracked and periodicity was detected by analyzing Fourier descriptors of the smoothed spatio-temporal curvature of point trajectories. Polana and Nelson [97] also used Fourier transform of reference trajectories of object regions, obtained by using normal flow, to recognize periodic activities. Seitz and Dyer [107] described affine invariant analysis of cyclic motion. They introduced period trace, which gave a strong response for signals that were projections of period signals. Ricquebourg and Bouthemy [102] differentiated between persons and vehicles by analyzing spatio-temporal signatures (projections) of each object. The idea being that the spatio-temporal signatures of people show periodicity. Cutler and Davis [23] presented an approach for detection of periodic motion as seen from a static camera. They computed object's self-similarity over time, which was periodic for periodic motions. Persons, Animals and cars were detected using this approach.This method was computationally expensive since a history of regions (segmented from images) needed to be saved and for each new image the segmented region is correlated with the history. Javed and Shah [52] introduced Recurrent Motion Images (RMI) to detect repetitive motion. These images were obtained by iteratively performing the exclusive-or operation and adding the scale and motion compensated silhouettes of objects. Large values in the RMIs indicated repetitive motion. This method was computationally efficient and therefore suitable for real time categorization tasks.

One limitation of all the above mentioned methods is that object trajectory information is required to compute periodicity, thus any errors in tracking will also show up in classification. In addition, this approach is not extendable for further categorization of the objects that exhibit non-periodic motion.

3.3.2 Object Categorization using Supervised Classifiers

In recent years, considerable progress has been made for detection of faces and pedestrians through supervised classification methods. Basically, these methods consist of learning classifier functions from training examples, where the functions map features from the image space to the object labels. In this context, a variety of approaches have been used including naive Bayes classifiers [106], Support Vector Machines (SVMs) [94] and Adaboost [125]. Specifically for surveillance related scenarios, Adaboost [34] is particularly suitable since it has been demonstrated to give high detection rates using simple Haar-like features in real-time [125]. Boosting is a machine learning method, that combines simple (base) classifiers into a single classifier that is more accurate than any one of the simple rules.

We now discuss the limitations of the supervised classification approaches, since these approaches are most commonly used to tackle the object categorization problem.

- Requirement of large number of training samples: Extremely large number of training examples are required to ensure good performance in the test phase. For example, Zhang et al. [130] used around 11000 positive and a 100000 negative labeled images for face detection, while Viola et al. [124] used 4916 positive and 10000 negative examples in their face detection framework. Obviously, manually marking such a large number of images is an arduous task.

- Not adaptive to change in viewing conditions: In supervised classification methods, the classifier parameters are fixed in the test stage. However, it is preferable to have a system that adapts itself to changing conditions in a particular scenario.

3.3.3 Object Categorization using Weakly Supervised Classifiers

One possible way around the requirement of a large labeled training set is to learn from unlabeled data. A number of methods have been developed by the machine learning community for training of classifiers using unlabeled data[62, 87, 10, 17]. The use of both labeled and unlabeled data for solving classification tasks was introduced by Nigam et. al. [87] in the area of text and information retreival. They employed the EM algorithm to infer the missing labels of the unlabeled data. The EM algorithm assigns labels to those unlabeled examples which are unambiguous. These new examples are used to update the the class density estimates, which then allows for the labeling of additional unlabeled examples. The basic assumption underlying the success of EM for this task is that the distribution of unlabeled data respects the class boundaries of the labeled data. Such an approach basically assumes that the density of unlabeled examples must be low near the classification boundary. This makes good sense for problems where the classes are Gaussian or are generated by some other simple density function. However, this assumption often does not hold for image based object detection tasks, where the density of the required class often cannot be modelled by simple parametric models.

The co-training approach to learn from unlabeled data was proposed by Blum and Mitchell [10]. The basic idea is to train classifiers on two independent "views" (features) of the same data, using a relatively small number of examples. Then to use each classifier's prediction on the unlabeled examples to enlarge the training set of the other. One advantage of this scheme is that it can be employed by discriminative classification approaches like boosting as well as generative approaches. Blum and Mitchell prove that co-training can find a very accurate classification rule, starting from a small quantity of labeled data if the two feature sets are statistically independent. However, this assumption does not hold in many realistic scenarios [96]. Recently, Balcan et al. [6] have shown that independence between the two views of the data is not a necessary assumption for co-training, instead weekly correlated views can also be used for co-training.

Levin et al. [73] use the co-training framework, in the context of boosted binary classifiers. Two boosted classifiers are employed for co-training. If one classifier predicts a label for a certain example with a high confidence then that labeled example is added to the training set of the other, otherwise the example is ignored. One of the two boosted classifiers employed for co-training uses background subtracted image regions, while the other classifier is trained on the image grey-levels directly. Note that the features are closely related. However, their approach empirically demonstrates that co-training is still possible even in the case the independence assumption does not hold. The co-training based learning approach have also been used successfully for text retrieval and classification by Collins and Singer [18]. They employed a boosting method that builds two classifiers in parallel from labeled and unlabeled data. The algorithm is iterative. In each iteration one of the classifier is updated while other is kept fixed. The algorithm is stopped when the error on the training data falls below a threshold.

3.4 Overview of the proposed categorization approach

In this chapter, we propose a *co-training* based approach to continuously label incoming data and use it for online update of the boosted classifier that was initially trained from a small labeled example set . One important point to note is that co-training is not a classification framework. It is actually a training method from unlabeled data. Co-training requires two separate views of the data for labeling, however a better classification decision can be made by combining the two views of data by a fully trained classifier. Thus, co-training is used to train a classifier in an *offline* setting. Once training is complete the combined view is used to make classification decisions.

The principal contribution of our approach is that it is an *online* method, in which separate views (features) of the data are used for co-training, while the combined view is used to make classification decisions in a single framework. To achieve this, we have exploited the fact that the the boosted classifier is a linear combination of simpler 'base' classifiers and that the adaptive boosting selection mechanism discourages redundancy among the selected features. The co-training is performed through the base classifiers, i.e., if a particular unlabeled example is labeled very confidently by a subset of the base classifiers (consisting of either the appearance based classifiers or the motion based classifiers) then it is used to update both the base classifiers and the boosting parameters using an online variant of the multi-class adaboost.M1 algorithm [93] . Note that, only few of the observed examples might qualify for co-training. Meanwhile the classification decision for each example is made by the boosted classifier, whose parameters have been updated from the labeled examples observed so far. The advantage of this approach is that the classifier is attuned to the characteristics of a particular scene. A classifier trained to give the best average performance in a variety of scenarios will usually be less accurate for a particular scene as compared to a classifier trained specifically for that scene. Obviously, the specific classifier would not perform well in other scenarios and thus it will not have widespread application. Our proposed approach tackles this dilemma by using a classifier trained on a general scenario that can automatically label examples observed in a specific scene and use them to fine tune its parameters online.

For our proposed approach, we demonstrate the performance of the classifier in the context of detection of pedestrians and vehicles observed through fixed cameras. Initially, the classifier is learned with a small number of labeled examples in a training phase. Both motion and appearance features are used for classification. These

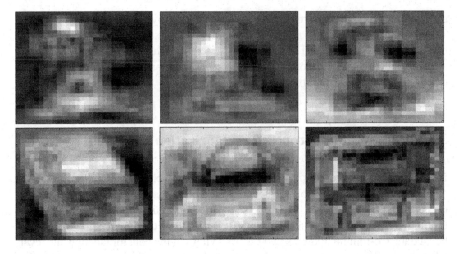

Fig. 3.1 First Row: The top 3 eigenvectors for the pedestrian subspace. Second Row: The top 3 eigenvectors for the vehicle subspace.

features are derived from Principal Component Analysis of the the optical flow and the appearance templates of the training examples. The classifier is continually updated online from unlabeled data during deployment. In order to make the detection system run in realtime, we use a background model (see Chapter 2) to select regions of interest in the scene. The boosted classifier searches within these regions and classifies the data into pedestrians, vehicles and non-stationary background. Co-training decisions are made at the base classifier level, and both the base classifiers and the boosting parameters are updated online. In the next Section, we discuss the features used for object representation and the base classifiers learned from these features.

3.5 Feature Selection and Base Classifiers

Selection of appropriate features for classification is important as the performance of the classifier is greatly affected by the feature used for object representation [72]. One approach for object representation in boosted classifiers is to use local Haar like features . The advantage of using the Haar features is that they can be calculated very efficiently [124]. However, it has been shown, in the context of face detection, by Zhang et al. [130] that base classifiers trained using global features are more reliable and the resulting boosted classifier has a higher detection rate. The drawback is that global features are usually more expensive to compute. However, in our approach, background subtraction is used to discard most of the stationary regions in an image before further processing, therefore we can afford to use global features for classification and still handle real-time processing requirements.

We employ both motion and appearance features for classification. The appearance of objects is represented by the gradient magnitude of the image regions occupied by the object. The gradient magnitude is computed as $\sqrt{f_x^2 + f_y^2}$, where f_x and f_y are horizontal and vertical gradients of the image respectively. Motion features have historically been used to recognize activities [29, 30]. We believe that the motion can effectively be employed for pedestrian and vehicle detection. Walking people undergo non-rigid deformations and have motion characteristics very different from the moving vehicles, which are rigid bodies. The motion is measured in terms of dense optical flow of regions. Optical flow describes the speed and direction of each pixel in the region. We use the algorithm by Lucas and Kanade [78] to obtain optical flow of the training examples of cars, vehicles and background regions.

We employ Principal Component Analysis (PCA) to obtain the motion and appearance subspaces . The appearance principal component model is formed by taking m example gradient magnitude images of dimensionality d in a column vector format, subtracting the mean, and computing the $d \times d$ dimensional covariance matrix C. The covariance matrix is then diagonalized via an eigenvalue decomposition $C = \Phi E \Phi^T$, where Φ is the eigenvector matrix and E is the corresponding diagonal matrix of its eigenvalues. Only m eigenvectors, corresponding to the m largest eigenvalues are used to form a projection matrix S_m to a lower dimension subspace. The motion subspace is computed similarly by vectorizing the optical flow estimates.

We construct a pedestrian appearance subspace with a $d \times m_1$ dimensional projection matrix S_{m_1} and a vehicle appearance subspace with a $d \times m_2$ dimensional projection matrix S_{m_2} by performing PCA on the respective training images. The parameters m_1 and m_2 are chosen such that the eigenvectors account for 99% of the variance in pedestrian and vehicle appearance data respectively. The top three eigenvectors for the pedestrians and vehicles are shown in Figure 3.1. The features for the base learners are obtained by projecting each training example $\mathbf{r}$ in the two subspaces and obtaining a feature vector $\mathbf{v} = [v_1, \ldots, v_{m_1}, v_{m_1+1}, \ldots, v_{m_1+m_2}]$, where

$$\left[v_1, \ldots, v_{m_1} \right] = \mathbf{r}^T \mathbf{S}_{m_1},$$
$$\left[v_{m_1+1}, \ldots, v_{m_1+m_2} \right] = \mathbf{r}^T \mathbf{S}_{m_2}.$$

The motion subspaces are constructed similarly from the m_3 and m_4 dimensional optical flow data respectively. We construct each base classifier from a single subspace coefficient. Thus we will have a total of $m_1 + m_2 + m_3 + m_4$ base classifiers. The top three eigenvectors for the pedestrians motion subspace are shown in Figure 3.2.

We use the Bayes classifier as our base classifier. Let c_1, c_2 and c_3 represent the pedestrian, vehicle and the non-stationary background classes respectively. The classification decision by the qth base classifier is taken as c_i if $P(c_i|v_q) > P(c_j|v_q)$ for all $j \neq i$. The posterior is given by the Bayes rule, i.e., $P(c_i|v_q) = \frac{p(v_q|c_i)P(c_i)}{p(v_q)}$. The pdf $p(v_q|c_i)$ is approximated through smoothed 1D histogram of the of the qth subspace coefficients obtained from the training data. The denominator $p(v_q)$ is

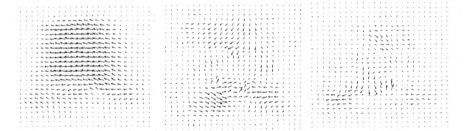

Fig. 3.2 The top 3 eigenvectors for the pedestrian optical flow subspace.

calculated as $\Sigma_{i=1}^{3} p(v_q|c_i) p(v_q)$. Note that the sum of posterior probabilities over all classes for a particular coefficient instance is one, i.e., for the three class case, $\Sigma_{i=1}^{3} P(c_i|v_q) = 1$.

Once the base classifiers are learned, the next step is to train the boosted classifier from the initial set of labeled data. In the next section, we discuss the co-training framework for augmenting the initial training set.

3.6 The Co-Training Framework

Boosting is an iterative method of finding a very accurate classifier by combining many base classifiers, each of which may only be moderately accurate . In the training phase of the Adaboost algorithm, the first step is to construct an initial distribution of weights over the training set. Then the boosting mechanism selects a base classifier that gives the least error, where the error is proportional to the weights of the misclassified data. Next, the weights associated with the data misclassified by the selected base classifier are increased and the process is repeated. Thus the algorithm encourages the selection of another classifier that performs better on the misclassified data in subsequent iterations. If the base classifiers are constructed such that each classifier is associated with a different feature, then the boosting mechanism will tend to select features that are not completely correlated. Note that, for co-training we require two classifiers trained on separate features of the same data. In our case, individual base classifiers either represent motion features or appearance features. Thus, if the subset of base classifier selected through the boosting mechanism, representing only motion (or only appearance) features, *confidently* predicts the label of the data, then we can add this data to our training set to update the rest of the classifiers. The confidence thresholds for the base classifiers can be determined through the training data or by using a small validation set.

Suppose H_N is the strong classifier learned through the Adaboost.M1 [34] algorithm . Let h_j, where $j \in \{1, \ldots, N\}$, be the base classifiers selected by the boosting algorithm. In order to set confidence thresholds on the labels given the base classifiers, we use a validation set of labeled images. For the class c_i, the confidence threshold T_{j,c_i}^{base} is set to be the highest posterior probability achieved by a negative example. This means that all examples in the validation set labeled as c_i by h_j with a probability higher than T_{j,c_i}^{base} actually belong to the class c_i. Thus during the online phase of the classifier, any example which has a probability higher than T_{j,c_i}^{base} is very likely to belong to the class c_i. The thresholds for all base classifiers selected by the boosting algorithm are similarly calculated.

Ideally, if a single base classifier confidently predicts a label with a probability higher than the established threshold then we should assume that the label is correct and use that example for further training the classifier. However, training from only a few wrongly labeled examples can severely degrade the performance of the classifier. Therefore, we choose to be more conservative and only select an unlabeled example if k, where $k \approx .2N$, base classifiers, where all of these classifiers are either appearance based or motion based, to confidently label an example.

It would be very inefficient to use every confidently labeled example for online training. The example labeled through co-training will improve the performance of the boosted classifier only if it has a small or negative margin, i.e., if the example lies close to the decision boundary in the solution space. If the example has been labeled unambiguously by the boosted classifier, i.e., it has a large margin, then using it for training will have little effect on the boosted classifier. Thus, we need unlabeled examples which have a small (or negative) margin and are also confidently labeled by the base classifiers. The limits on the score of the boosted classifier can also be established through the validation set. The score of an example for the label c_i is computed by Adaboost.M1 as $\Sigma_{n:h_n(x)=c_i} log(\frac{1}{\beta_n})$, where β_n is the coefficient of the nth classifier selected by the algorithm. The label that gets the highest score is assigned to the example. For the class c_i, the threshold to determine the usefulness of employing the example for retraining, i.e., T_{j,c_i}^{base}, is set to be the highest normalized score achieved by a negative example. Thus an example, assigned the label c_i by base classifiers should only be used for retraining if it gets a score of less than T_{j,c_i}^{base} by the boosted classifier.

Once an example has been labeled and if it has a small margin, the next issue is to use this example for updating the boosting parameters and the base classifiers online. The co-training and online updation algorithm is given in Figure 3.3.

3.6.1 Online Learning

Note that an online algorithm does not need to 'look at' all the training data at once, rather it process each training instance without the need for storage and maintains a current hypothesis that has been learned from the training examples encountered so far. To this end we use an online boosting algorithm proposed by Oza and Russel [93]. The inputs to the algorithm are the current boosted classifier H_N, the constituent base classifiers, and parameters λ_n^{sc} and λ_n^{sw}, where $n = 1, \ldots, N$. λ_n^{sc} and λ_n^{sw} are the sums of the weights of the correctly classified and misclassified examples, respectively, for each of the N base classifiers.

Online Co-Train   -if atleast k motion based or appearance based classifiers confidently predict a label c_p for incoming example x, where $p \in \{1, \ldots, numclasses\}$, then

- if $\left(\left(\sum_{n:h_n(x)=c_p} log(\frac{1}{\beta_n}) \right) / \left(\sum_{n=1}^{N} log(\frac{1}{\beta_n}) \right) \right) < T_{c_p}^{ada}$

  - $\beta_n \leftarrow OnlineBoosting(H_N, x, c_p)$
  - add example with assigned label c_i to the validation set.
  - for $j = 1, \ldots, N$
    - for $i = 1, \ldots, numclasses$
      - T_{j,c_i}^{base}=max posterior probability, for class c_i by h_j, of a negative example in the validation set
  - for $i = 1, \ldots, numclasses$
    - $T_{c_i}^{ada}$=max H_N normalized score, for class c_i, of a negative example in the validation set

---

— returns B_n:**OnlineBoost($\mathbf{H_N, x, label}$)**
-Set the example's initial weight $\lambda_x = 1$.
- For each base model h_n,in the boosted classifier

1. Set z by sampling Poisson(λ_x).
2. Do z times : $h_n \leftarrow OnlineBase(h_n, x, label)$
3. if $h_n(x)$ is the correct label,

- $\lambda_n^{sc} = \lambda_n^{sc} + \lambda_x$, $\varepsilon_n = \frac{\lambda_n^{sw}}{\lambda_n^{sc} + \lambda_n^{sw}}$, $\lambda_x = \lambda_x \left(\frac{1}{2(1-\varepsilon_n)} \right)$

4. else

- $\lambda_n^{sw} = \lambda_n^{sw} + \lambda_x$, $\varepsilon_n = \frac{\lambda_n^{sw}}{\lambda_n^{sc} + \lambda_n^{sw}}$, $\lambda_x = \lambda_x \left(\frac{1}{2(\varepsilon_n)} \right)$

5. calculate $\beta_n = log(\frac{1-\varepsilon_n}{\varepsilon_n})$

Fig. 3.3 The co-training method. Note that both T^{base} and T^{ada} are automatically computed from the validation set. The subfunction $onlineboost()$ was proposed in [93]. λ_n^{sc} are sum of weights for examples that were classified correctly by the base model at the stage n while λ_n^{sw} is sum for incorrectly classified examples.

The main idea of the algorithm is to update each base classifier and the associated boosting parameter using the incoming example. The example is assigned a weight λ at the start of the algorithm. For the first iteration, the base classifier is updated z times, where $z = Poisson(\lambda)$. Then, if h_1 misclassifies the example, λ_1^{sw} is updated which is the sum of weight of all incorrectly classified examples by h_1. The weight of the example λ is increased and it is presented to the next base classifier. Note that in the regular 'batch' adaboost method the weight of the example is also increased in case of misclassification. However, all the weights are assumed to be known at the next iteration. In the online boosting method only the sums of weights of correctly classified and misclassified examples (see so far) are available. The boosting parameters, β_n, are also updated using these weights. Note that the algorithm also needs to update the base classifiers online. Since our base classifiers are represented as normalized histograms, they can easily be updated, i.e., the training example is added to the histogram representing the probability distribution of the feature, and the histogram is re-normalized. The online learning algorithm is shown in the bottom half of Figure 3.3.

3.7 Co-Training Ability Measurement

We used Collaborative Ability (CA) Measurement [112] to determine the effectiveness of co-training framework in current setup of object classification . CA indicates whether two classifiers can co-train effectively. It quantifies the degree by which one classifier can reduce the classification uncertainty of other classifier. If CA is high than there is large portion of data for which one classifier is very confident and can provide such data to the other classifier and help improve its performance. Data predicted by a classifier is categorized in two sets: *Certainty Set (CSet)* are those instances for which a classifier can predict the label with a confidence that is higher than some predetermined threshold and *Uncertainty Set (UCSet)* are those instances for which the confidence of classifier's prediction is below some predetermined threshold. Formally CA between two classifiers h_1 and h_2 is computed as:

$$N_1 = | CSet(h_1) \cap UCSet(h_2) |,$$
$$N_2 = | UCSet(h_1) \cap CSet(h_2) |,$$
$$N_3 = | CSet(h_1) \cap CSet(h_2) |,$$
$$N_4 = | UCSet(h_1) \cap UCSet(h_2) |,$$
$$CA_{h_1 h_2} = \frac{N_1 + N_2}{N_1 + N_2 + N_3 + N_4}. \tag{3.1}$$

A value of the CA measure greater than zero indicates that the two classifiers can benefit from co-training. Further discussion on this measure is carried out in the next section.

3.8 Results

For the initial training of the multi-category classifier, we used 50 training images per class. Images of pedestrians and vehicles from a variety of poses were used. For the non-stationary background class, we selected the scenarios where the background modelling is likely to fail, for example sporadically moving tree branches, or waves in a pond. All extracted objects were scaled to the same size (30x30 pixels). Features were obtained by projecting all the image regions in the pedestrian and vehicle subspaces. The base and boosted classifier thresholds were determined for a validation set consisting of 20 images per class for a total of 60 images.

Table 3.1 The collaborative ability (CA) measure values for the three sequences. The CA measure ranges between zero and one.

Sequence #	CA value
1	.31
2	.18
3	.25

We evaluated our algorithm for person and vehicle detection in three different locations. In each location, the view consisted of the road, with walkways near by. The pedestrian and vehicular traffic along the paths was fairly consistent. First, we calculated the collaborative ability measure for the three sequences by dividing them into training and testing sets. Table 3.1) shows collaborative ability values obtained for the three sequences. The measure was well above zero for all sequences indicating that improved performance through co-training is expected.

We demonstrated the improvement through online co-training at each location in two different ways. Firstly, we divided the sequences in equal size chunks and show that classification accuracy improves with time though online learning. Figure 3.4 first column shows classification results over two minute subsets for the three sequences. Note that with the exception of one interval in the second sequence, the performance either consistently improves with time or remains stable. The performance measure was the classification accuracy, i.e., the percentage of the number of valid vehicle and pedestrian detections to the total number of detections.

For further analysis of the method, we divided each sequence into two sets. In the first set the classification results were obtained using the multi-class Adaboost.M1 classifier without co-training. Then the other set was run with the co-trainable classifier, stopping when a pre-determined number of labeled examples had updated the classifier parameters. Once the updated parameters were obtained, the boosting algorithm was re-run on the first sequence with the classifier parameters frozen and the change in performance was measured. The improvement in the performance of the algorithm in the first setup is shown in Figure 3.4 second column. The horizontal axis shows the number of examples obtained through co-training from the second sequence, and the vertical axis shows the detection rates on the test sequence. The detection rates improve significantly even with a small number of new training examples. Since the automatically labeled training examples are from the specific scene on which the classifier is being evaluated on, only a few co-trained examples are sufficient to increase the detection accuracy. The classification accuracy was relatively low for sequence 2 since there was persistent occlusion between vehicles. Detection results for the three sequences are shown in Figures 3.5, 3.6 and 3.7.

Upon analysis of the examples selected for co-training by the base classifiers we found out that approximately 96% of these were correctly labeled. The small number of mis-classification were caused mainly by occlusion. One important point in the use of examples obtained through co-training for update of classifier parameters is that, if the examples are misaligned, or the target object is only partially visible, then updating the classifier parameters with that example can lower the classifica-

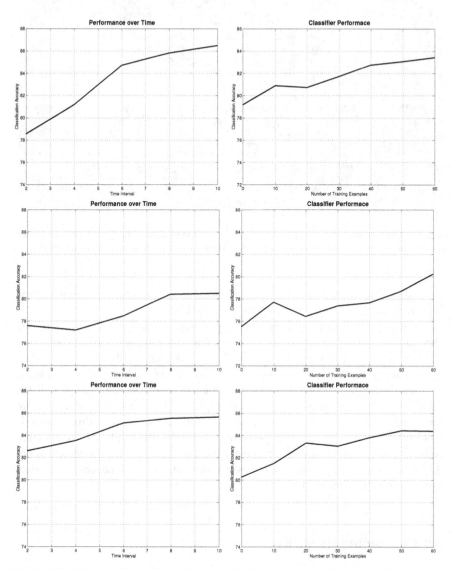

Fig. 3.4 First Column: Change in performance with increase in time for sequence 1,2 and 3 respectively. The performance was measured over two minute intervals. Approximately 150 to 200 possible detections of vehicles or pedestrians were made in each time interval. Second Column: Performance vs. the number of co-trained examples, for sequences 1,2 and 3 respectively. The graphs for each sequence show the improvement in performance with the increase in the use of examples labeled by the co-training method.

tion accuracy. We reduce the likelihood of such a scenario by forcing the detected region to be within the foreground regions as determined by the background mod-

Fig. 3.5 Some classification results from sequence 1. Objects classified as pedestrians are shown in black bounding boxes and objects classified as vehicles are shown in white bounding boxes.

eling algorithm. Moreover we only select those examples that are at peaks of the (boosted) classifier scoring function, as suggested in [73].

Another problem that might arise during co-training is that if examples of one class are observed in much greater numbers than other classes. Updating the classifier parameters by training through examples of one class only can bias the classifier. This problem always occurs in a scenario when the background has to be distinguished from the object by the classifier. In this case, the examples of the background class outnumber by far the examples of the object class. Since, we are removing most of the background region by background subtraction, this scenario is less likely to occur. To avoid this problem completely, if examples of one class are being confidently labeled in much greater number than others, then one can store the examples and sample them in numbers comparable to other classes, rather than using all of them for training.

3.9 Concluding Remarks

In this chapter, we presented a unified boosting based framework for online detection and categorization of objects. The examples that were confidently labeled by a small subset of base classifiers were used to update both the boosting coefficients and the base classifiers. We have demonstrated that a classifier's performance can be significantly improved just by using a small numbers of examples from the specific scenario in which the classifier is employed. This is because the variation in the poses of objects, backgrounds and illumination conditions in a specific scene is far less than the possible variation in all possible detection scenarios. The use of co-training in an online classification framework allows us to focus on the specific

Fig. 3.6 Moving object classification results from sequence 2. Objects classified as pedestrians are shown in black bounding boxes and objects classified as vehicles are shown in white bounding boxes.

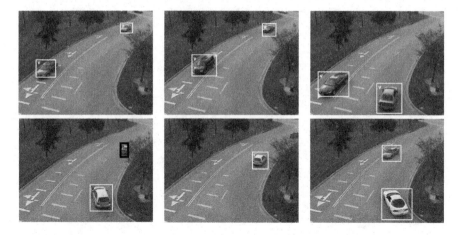

Fig. 3.7 Moving object classification results from sequence 3. Black bounding boxes indicate objects classified as pedestrians. Note that in row 2, first image the car has been misclassified due to occlusion from the tree branches.

subset of poses and backgrounds likely to be viewed in each scenario, thus greatly improving the classification performance.

Chapter 4
OBJECT TRACKING IN A SINGLE CAMERA

4.1 Introduction

The goal of tracking is to determine the position and motion of objects in a sequence of images . If the objects are continuously observable and their shape, size or motion do not vary over time then tracking is not a hard problem. However, in realistic environments, none of these assumptions hold true. Objects do undergo occlusion, that is, another object or structure blocks the view of the objects. Therefore, observations of the objects are not continuously available. Objects, specially people undergo a change in shape while moving. In addition, their motion is not constant. Both people and vehicles can accelerate, de-accelerate or make a complete change in their direction of motion. Thus, tracking in realistic scenarios is a hard problem. We formulate the object tracking problem as region tracking, where regions are 2D projections of objects on the image plane. We assume that regions can enter and exit the view space. They can undergo a change in motion and they can also get occluded by the other regions.

We report the related work in Section 4.2. We point out the issues that any tracking algorithm needs to deal with, in Section 4.3. Our approach to the tracking problem is presented [52, 56] in Section 4.4. The results and future work are discussed in Sections 4.5 and 4.6 respectively.

4.2 Related Work

The methods to solve the single camera tracking problem can be divided into a number of categories depending upon exactly what is being tracked. These categories are discussed in the following sections.

O. Javed, M. Shah, *Automated Multi-Camera Surveillance: Algorithms and Practice*, 45
DOI: 10.1007/978-0-387-78881-4_4, © Springer Science+Business Media, LLC 2008

4.2.1 Feature Point Tracking Methods

The feature tracking methods assume that measurements of certain features are available over time . The measurements are of fixed length, i.e., the dimensionality of the measurement vector does not change over time. The task is to establish correspondence between measurements, i.e., to determine if the measurements taken at different times originate from the same feature. Measurements can be spurious, i.e., they originate from noisy sensor rather than an actual geometric feature. In addition, occlusion can take place between the features resulting in the loss of measurements for some features. Both deterministic and statistical approaches have been proposed to solve these problems.

4.2.1.1 Deterministic Methods

The point feature is the simplest feature to track. A number of approaches have been proposed to solve the point correspondence problem with deterministic algorithms. Sethi and Jain [108] used a greedy exchange (GE) algorithm to minimize a cost function for tracking. The cost function was based on motion smoothness constraint, i.e., minimal change in velocity was assumed. The GE algorithm assumed that the correspondence between the first two frames was known. Rangarajan and Shah [100] proposed the proximal uniformity constraint to perform motion correspondence. The assumption was that points followed smooth paths and covered small distances in small time intervals. A non-iterative greedy algorithm was used to assign correspondences. This algorithm allowed for occlusion and for missing point detection but did not allow for false detections. Chetverikov and Verestoy [16] also used the smoothness constraint for tracking by a three step algorithm. In the first step, the initial correspondence between points in the first three frames is established. In the second step tracking is performed in the subsequent frames. Trajectories broken due to long occlusions are connected in the third step. Veenman et. al. [123] introduced individual, combined and global motion models for establishing point correspondences. The individual motion model represented the motion of individual points. The combined motion model enforced the motion smoothness constraint over the complete set of points. The global motion model extended the smoothness constraint over the whole sequence. The authors also presented an optimal greedy algorithm that assigns the correspondences by using the aforementioned motion models. The algorithm allowed for occlusion, entries, exits and false detection of point features.

4.2.1.2 Statistical Methods

The best known statistical approach for tracking is the Multiple Hypothesis Tracker (MHT) [22] . The MHT attempts to match a variable number of feature points globally while allowing for missing or false detection. At each time instant MHT maintains a set of current hypothesis. Each hypothesis represents a different set of assignments of measurements to features, i.e., it is a collection of disjoint tracks, where a track is defined as a sequence of measurements that are assumed to originate from the same physical entity. Each hypothesis predicts the location of a set of expected entity features and these are compared with actual measurements in the next frame on the basis of Mahalanobis distance. This approach is computationally expensive, though real time approximations have been proposed [105]. There is a class of suboptimal methods that require constant computation for establishing correspondence over a fixed set of frames. The Joint Probability Data Association Filter (JPDAF) considers the possibility of all measurements originating from any feature. It assumes that the number of features to be tracked is known *a priori*. Thus it cannot deal with entrance and exits of features. There is a large amount of literature on data association. The standard text is by Bar-Shalom and Fortmann [7]. In order to enable JPDAF to perform tracking in an environment, where exits and entries of features are possible, methods combining JPDAF and multi-hypothesis tracker have also been proposed by Bar-Shalom et. al. [28].

People, as opposed to points, are projected as regions on the image plane. Each region is composed of a certain number of pixels. The size and shape of regions can change over time, thus feature correspondence algorithms are not ideally suited to track people.

4.2.2 Region Tracking Methods

The region tracking algorithms can be loosely divided into two main groups . The algorithms that track the boundary or contour of the target region and the algorithms that track the appearance of the region. Usually the later methods do not explicitly track the change in shape of the region, rather a fixed shape appearance model is used for tracking. Recently algorithms have been proposed that combine these two approaches. Below, we will discuss each category of the region tracking methods in detail.

4.2.2.1 Contour Trackers (SNAKES)

A snake is an elastic curve that is fitted to the detected features of a region . The fitting is done through an energy minimization function which draws the curve towards the features. One of the most commonly used features is the edge map of the image. The constraints of smoothness and continuity are imposed on the curves. A large amount of research has been conducted on contour trackers. The seminal work on snakes was by Kass et. al. [65]. Williams and Shah [127] presented a greedy algorithm for contour fitting. Bouthemy et.al [102] used spatio-temporal XT slices from the image sequence volume for tracking regions. The XT trajectories were extracted as contour tracks over successive XY images. An extensive treatment of the subject is provided by Isard and Blake [9]. Contours can also be tracked by representing them as evolving wavefronts using partial differential equations [95], [8]. More details on variational methods for tracking can be obtain from the text by Sethian [109].

4.2.2.2 Appearance Trackers

These trackers model the appearance of the target object. Comaniciu et. al [20],[21] proposed a mean shift approach for region tracking . The task of finding the region in current frame was formulated as follows: the feature representing the color or texture of the target region being tracked was assumed to have a density function, while a candidate region also had a feature distributed by a certain density. The problem was to find a candidate region whose associated density is most similar to the target density. A modified Bhattacharraya coefficient measure was used as a distance metric between the distributions. The approach adopted by Jepson et. al [61] involved appearance models learned over time, along with motion information and an outlier modeling process. An online EM-algorithm was used to adapt the appearance model parameters over time. One major shortcoming of the appearance trackers is that they cannot adjust to large changes in scale or shape of the target region.

4.2.3 Methods to Track People

People tracking approaches exploit the shape and motion of human body to achieve correspondence. Some trackers attempt to track the complete human body using body models, i.e., tracking limbs, head and torso . Other approaches attempt to track the projected 2D silhouette of body. Surveys by Aggarwal and Cai [4], Gavrilla [36], and Moeslund et al. [85] provide a detailed overview of human motion tracking and analysis. Here we give a brief description of the person tracking approaches.

4.2.3.1 Model-Based Person Tracking

The human body model usually consists of connected cylinders or Gaussians. Rohr [104] found the outline of human body by Eigen vector line-fitting and then fitted the 2D projection to the 3D model by minimizing a distance measure. Rehg et. al [15] used the Multiple Hypothesis approach to fit the silhouette information to a 2D prismatic body model. Deutscher et. al. [25] used the particle filtering approach to fit edge and silhouette features to a body model.

The problem of full body tracking is very difficult. The reasons being non-linear motion, dynamic shapes changes, and constant self occlusion between human body parts. Good tracking results have only been obtained in very controlled circumstances, i.e., tracking a single person walking fairly close to the camera, and most of the above mentioned approaches require manual initialization. Thus these approaches are not suitable for use in automated surveillance systems.

4.2.3.2 2D Tracking of Person Silhouette

For automated surveillance systems, tracking is usually carried out on foreground regions obtained by the background subtraction process. Azerbayejani et. al. [128] proposed region tracking using probabilistic models of human body. A single human body was tracked by fitting a mixture of Gaussian to the silhouette. The method doesn't deal with tracking of multiple humans. W4 [41] used template matching with 2nd order motion prediction for tracking regions. The templates were constructed by combining the gray scale textural appearance and shape information of person together in a single template. These templates were also used to resolve the correspondence after occlusion. Multiple people in a single foreground region were detected by finding peaks in the silhouette and in the vertical projection. Khan and Shah [67] used a mixture of Gaussians in spatial and color space to track people. Each person upon its entry was segmented into a set of classes by fitting a Gaussian mixture model, using the EM algorithm. In subsequent frames, a class label was assigned to each pixel by computing the probability of that pixel belonging to each of the existing classes and picking the maximum probability. Tao et. al. [132] used Kalman filter and region correlation to establish correspondence. Elgammal et. al. [31] modeled the color of the people by kernel density estimates. The shape was modeled by training three Gaussian distributions,where there Gaussians modeled the head,torso and legs of the person. The correspondences were assigned using the maximum likelihood approach. The above mentioned methods assumed that a single person cannot belong to multiple regions. McKenna et. al. [83] used only color histograms to track people. Heuristics were used to merge two regions close to each other, thus a single person could belong to two regions. Since no motion or shape model is being used, there is a high probability of error if objects are similarly colored.

4.3 Problems in Tracking 2D silhouettes of People

One of the major issues that a tracking algorithm needs to solve is tracking during occlusion. Another problem is the occurrence of simultaneous exit and entry of objects at the same scene location. We will now discuss these problems in detail.

4.3.1 Occlusion

Occlusion occurs when an object is not visible in an image because some other object/structure is blocking its view . Tracking objects under occlusion is difficult because accurate position and velocity of an occluded object cannot be determined. Different cases of occlusion are described in the following,

- Inter-object occlusion occurs when one object blocks the view of other objects in the field of view of the camera. The background subtraction method gives a single region for occluding objects. If two initially non-occluding objects cause occlusion then this condition can be easily detected. However, if objects enter the scene while occluding each other then it is difficult to determine if inter-object occlusion is occurring. The problem is to identify that the foreground region contains multiple objects and to determine the location of each object in the region. Since people usually move in groups, which results in frequent inter-object occlusion, therefore detecting and resolving inter-object occlusion is important for surveillance applications.
- Occlusion of objects due to scene structures causes the objects to disappear completely for a certain amount of time, that is there is no foreground region representing such objects. For example, a person walks behind a building, or a person enters a car. A decision has to be made whether to wait for reappearance of the objects, or determine that the object has exited the scene.

4.3.2 Entries and Exits

Detecting exit and entries is another problem in tracking objects for surveillance purposes. Entry is defined as an object entering the field of view of the camera. Entries and exits are easy to detect if (exiting and entering) objects are separate in the camera view. However, detecting an entry and an exit of two (or more objects) at the same place and at the same time is difficult . If one person enters the scene at a certain position while another person leaves from the same position at the same time then this scenario needs to be distinguished from the situation in which person moves right near the exit and then start moving in the direction it came from.

4.4 Proposed Approach for Tracking

4.4.1 Assumptions

We assume that the camera is stationary. We also assume that the frames are processed at a fast rate so that objects move a small distance between consecutive frames. We have observed that a frame processing rate of 10Hz or more is sufficient for tracking walking people. There are no restrictions on camera orientation. Camera calibration is also not required.

4.4.2 Object Tracker

The output of the background subtraction method (described in Chapter 2) for each frame is foreground regions R_i where $0 \leq i \leq L$ and L is the total number of regions. Each region R_i is a set of connected pixels. Note that, it is not valid to assume that regions correspond to objects. In case of occlusion multiple objects can belong to the same region. Also similarity in color between a object and background can result in splitting of that object's silhouette into multiple regions. Therefore, a model of object is required which can tolerate these split and merge cases.

Uninteresting objects like trees and flags can also show up as foreground regions for short periods of time. To prevent these objects from affecting the tracking results, we establish a minimum initial observation parameter, O_{min}. If a region disappears in less than O_{min} frames, then it is considered a false detection and its tracks are removed. Also, people can disappear in the middle of the frame, for example, background subtraction module might fail to extract a person or the person might walk behind a tree. We introduce the maximum missed observation parameter, M_{max}, to capture this situation. The track of a person is terminated if he or she is not observed in M_{max} frames.

An object, P_k, is modeled by color, spatial and motion models and its size, n_k, in terms of pixels. The shape is modeled by a Gaussian distribution, $s_k(x)$, with variance equal to the sample variance of the person silhouette. The color is modeled by a normalized histogram, $h_k(c(x))$, where the function $c(.)$ returns the color at pixel position x in the current frame. A linear velocity predictor is used to model the motion.

For each incoming frame, each pixel x_i, where $x_i \in R_i$, votes for the label of an object, for which the product of color and spatial probability is the highest, i.e.,

$$\arg\max_k (s_k(x)h_k(c(x))). \tag{4.1}$$

Now

- if the number of votes $V_{i,q}$, i.e., votes from R_i for P_k, are a significant percentage, say T, of n_k, i.e., $(V_{i,k}/n_k) > T$, and also $(V_{i,q}/n_q) < T$ where $k \neq q$, then all the pixels in R_i are used to update P_k's models. Incase more than one region satisfy this condition then all regions are used to update the object model. This case represents an object splitting into multiple regions.
- if $(V_{i,k}/n_k) > T$, and $(V_{i,q}/n_q) > T$ then this case represent two objects merging into a single region. In this case, only those pixels in R_i that voted for P_k will be used to update P_k's models.

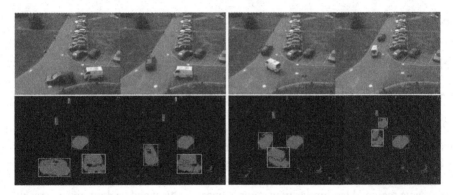

Fig. 4.1 PETS Dataset 1,test, camera 2 sequence (frames 2440-2580). The first row shows the images. The second row shows regions obtained by background subtraction along with their bounding boxes

- if $(V_{i,k}/n_k) < T$, $\forall i$, i.e., No observation matches the model k. This might be due to complete occlusion of the object or the object might have exit the frame. If position plus predicted velocity of the object is near the frame boundary, the object is determined to have exit the frame. Otherwise the mean of the spatial model is updated by linear velocity prediction. The rest of the parameters are kept constant.
- if $(V_{i,k}/n_k) < T$, $\forall k$, i.e., The region R_i does not match any model. This means it is a new entry. A new object model is created for this region.

4.5 Results

The tracking approach described in previous sections was applied to a large number of video sequences. It performed quite well, in particular it was able to deal with complicated occlusions between multiple people. The algorithm was also applied with just the spatial and motion model on the sequences provided for the purpose of performance evaluation of tracking in the "Second IEEE International Workshop on Performance Evaluation of Tracking and Surveillance, PETS 2001" [113]. Specifically the video sequences (dataset 1 test sequences 1 and 2) were used. The *PETS* sequences were JPEG compressed and therefore noisy. Each sequence consisted of 2688 frames. The sequences contained persons, groups or people walking together and vehicles. For each sequence, the background subtraction algorithm (described in Chapter 2) detects moving objects in the scene and calculates bounding box, centroid and correspondence of each object over the frames. Figure 4.1 shows interest region detection results on the PETS sequences. The tracking algorithm successfully handled occlusions between people, between vehicles and between people and vehicles as shown in Figure 4.2.

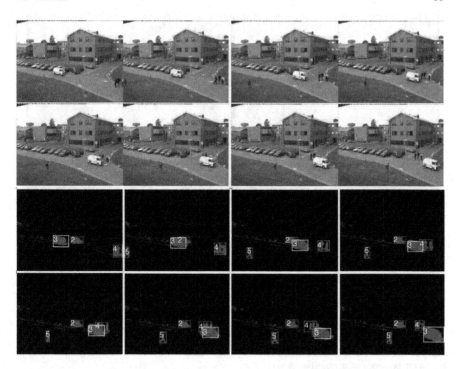

Fig. 4.2 Complicated occlusion example. The top two rows show the images from the sequence. The next two rows show the regions obtained from background subtraction and their bounding boxes. Notice that Occlusion between 2 cars and a group of people was handled successfully. PETS Data Set 1,Testing, Camera 1 sequence. Frames 795-940

Figure 4.3 shows tracking results on a person and a vehicle on sunny day. Note that there is strong lighting variation across the scene due to shadows of buildings and trees. Figure 4.4 shows tracking results for a sequence containing multiple people. Our tracker was able to track each person during partial occlusion. Correct tracking was also maintained through complete occlusion of people. The algorithm was also tested in the down town Orlando. Figure 4.5 shows tracking results on a cloudy day in down town orlando. The algorithm is successful in establishing correspondences in these varied conditions. Figure 4.6 shows a person being completely occluded by a bus. The predicted position of the person is near the frame boundary, therefore the person is determined to have exit the frame. Figure 4.7 shows tracking results in an indoor situation in which people are partially occluded by scene structure, i.e., a desk in this particular case.

We have tested our system in varying illumination conditions, with multiple people and vehicles in the scene, and in both indoor and outdoor scenarios. The above mentioned experiments clearly demonstrate that our algorithm is able to robustly track objects in a variety of circumstances. Please see Figure 6.2(b) (chapter 6) for analysis of tracking performance over six hours of video in realistic scenar-

Fig. 4.3 Orlando Down Town, Orange Ave. A person and a vehicle being tracked on a sunny day, i.e., in the presence of strong shadows.

ios. More results are available on http://www.cs.ucf.edu/$\sim$ vision/projects/Knight /KNIGHT.html.

4.6 Discussion

The proposed tracker is successful in resolving occlusions between people. However, it does make the assumption that there is no occlusion when a person model is initialized, i.e., when a person first appears in the camera view he/she is not undergoing occlusion. This assumption is reasonable only for a low density of traffic in the camera view. In most surveillance scenarios, there is a moderate to high density of people in the scene. People usually walk in groups in such a scenario. Thus, a tracker must have the ability to detect the number and position of people in a scene. In our opinion, people segmentation should use multiple cues including face location [129, 76] body shape [131], color of clothing, gradients at boundaries and the human body size information. However, with the current limitations on computing power, it might not be possible to fuse information from such a large number of cues for real time tracking.

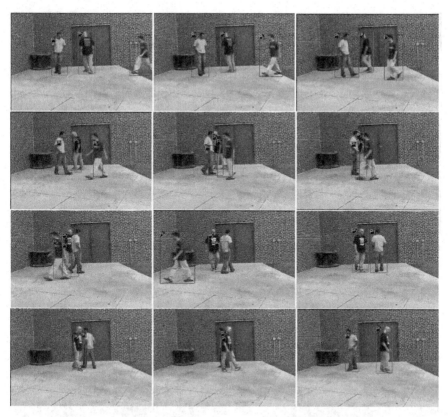

Fig. 4.4 Tracking results in a single camera. The tracker is capable of handling multiple occluded people.

Fig. 4.5 Orlando down town. Two persons being tracked on a cloudy day (low illumination).

Fig. 4.6 Orlando down town. A person being completely occluded by a bus. Since the position plus predicted velocity of the person is near the frame boundary, the person is determined to have exit the frame.

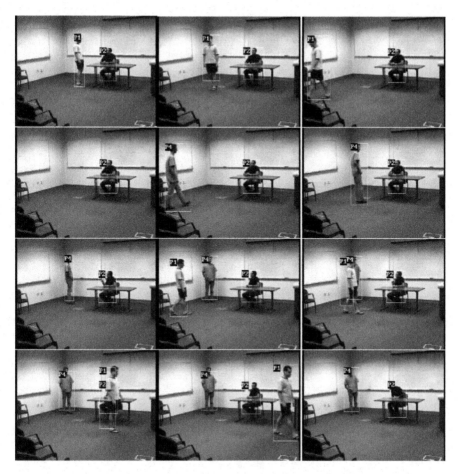

Fig. 4.7 Tracking results in an indoor environment. Note that location of object is estimated fairly accurately even during occlusion

Chapter 5
TRACKING IN MULTIPLE CAMERAS WITH DISJOINT VIEWS

5.1 Problem Overview and Key Challenges

In most cases, it is not possible for a single camera to observe the complete area of interest because sensor resolution is finite and structures in the scene limit the visible areas. Thus, multiple cameras are required to observe large environments. Even, in this case, it is usually not possible to completely cover large areas with cameras. Therefore in realistic scenarios, surveillance of wide areas requires a system with the ability to track objects while observing them through multiple cameras with non-overlapping field of views. Moreover, it is preferable that the tracking approach does not require camera calibration or complete site modelling since the luxury of calibrated cameras or site models is not available in most situations. Also, maintaining calibration between a large network of sensors is a daunting task, since a slight change in the position of a sensor will require the calibration process to be repeated. In this chapter, we present an algorithm that caters for all these constraints and tracks people across multiple un-calibrated cameras with non-overlapping field of views.

The task of a multi-camera tracker is to establish correspondence between observations across cameras. Multi-camera tracking specially across non-overlapping views is a challenging problem because of two reasons.

- The observations of an object are often widely separated in time and space, when viewed from non-overlapping cameras. Thus, unlike conventional single camera tracking approaches, proximity in space and time cannot be used to constrain possible correspondences.
- The appearance of an object in one camera view might be very different from its appearance in another camera view due to the differences in illumination, pose and camera properties.

In order to deal with the first problem, we assume that the tracks of individual cameras are available, and find the correspondences between these tracks in different cameras such that the corresponded tracks belong to same object in the real

O. Javed, M. Shah, *Automated Multi-Camera Surveillance: Algorithms and Practice*,
DOI: 10.1007/978-0-387-78881-4_5, © Springer Science+Business Media, LLC 2008

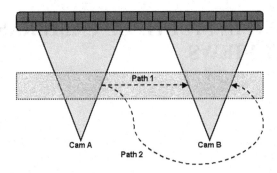

Fig. 5.1 The figure shows two possible paths an object can take from camera A to B.

world. We use the observations of people through the system of cameras to discover relationships between the cameras. For example, suppose two cameras A and B are successively arranged alongside a walkway, see Figure 5.1. Suppose people moving along one direction of the walkway that are initially observed in camera A are also observed entering camera B after a certain time interval. People can take many paths across A and B. However, due to physical and practical constraints, people will follow some paths more often then others. Thus, the locations of exits and entrances between cameras, direction of movement and the average time taken to reach from A to B can be used as cues to constrain correspondences. We refer to these cues as *space-time* cues and exploit these cues to learn the inter-camera relationships. The inter-camera relationships are learned in the form of a probability density function (pdf) of space time parameters (i.e., the probability of an object entering a certain camera at a certain time given the location, time and velocity of its exit from another camera) from the training data. Instead of imposing assumptions about the form of this pdf, we let the data 'speak for itself' ([70]) by estimating the pdf using kernel density estimators.

A commonly used cue for tracking in a single camera is the appearance of the objects. Appearance of an object can be modelled by its color or brightness histograms, and it is a function of scene illumination, object geometry, object surface material properties (e.g., surface albedo) and the camera parameters. Among all these, only the object surface material properties remain constant as an object moves across cameras. Thus, the color distribution of an object can be fairly different when viewed from two different cameras. One way to match appearances in different cameras is by finding a transformation that maps the appearance of an object in one camera image to its appearance in the other camera image. However, for a given pair of cameras, this transformation is not unique and also depends upon the scene illumination and camera parameters. In this chapter, we show that despite depending upon a large number of parameters, all such transformations lie in a low dimensional subspace for a given pair of cameras. The proposed method learns this subspace of mappings for each pair of cameras from the training data by using probabilistic principal component analysis. Thus, given appearances in two different cameras, and the subspace of brightness transfer functions learned during the training phase, we can estimate the probability that the transformation between the appearances lies in the learnt subspace.

We present an ML estimation framework to use these cues in a principled manner for tracking . The correspondence probability, i.e., the probability that two observations originate from the same object, depends on both the space-time information and the appearance. Tracks assignment is achieved by maximizing the correspondence likelihood . This is achieved by converting the ML estimation problem into a problem of finding the path cover of a directed graph for which an optimal solution can be efficiently obtained.

Our proposed inter-camera appearance and space-time relationship models for tracking that do not assume

- explicit camera calibration,
- a site model,
- presence of a single ground plane across cameras,
- a particular non-overlapping camera topology,
- constant illumination, or
- constant camera parameters, for example, focal length or exposure.

In the next section, we discuss related research. In Section 5.3, a probabilistic formulation of the problem is presented. Learning of inter-camera spatio-temporal and appearance relationships is discussed in Sections 5.4 and 5.5 respectively. In Section 5.6, a maximum likelihood solution to find correspondences is given. Results are presented in Section 5.7.

5.2 Related Work

In general, multi-camera tracking methods differ from each other on the basis of their assumption of overlapping or non-overlapping views, explicit calibration vs learning the inter-camera relationship, type of calibration, use of 3D position of objects, and/or features used for establishing correspondences. Here, we organize the multi-camera tracking literature into two major categories based on the requirement of overlapping or non-overlapping views.

5.2.1 Multi-Camera Tracking Methods Requiring Overlapping Views:

A large amount of work on multi-camera surveillance assumes overlapping views. Jain and Wakimoto [51] used calibrated cameras and an environmental model to obtain 3D location of a person. The fact that multiple views of the same person are mapped to the same 3D location was used for establishing correspondence. Cai and Aggarwal [13], used multiple calibrated cameras for surveillance. Geometric and intensity features were used to match objects for tracking. These features were modeled as multi-variate Gaussians and the Mahalanobis distance measure was used for matching. Chang and Gong [119] used the top most point on an object detected in one camera to compute its associated epipolar line in other cameras. The distance between the epipolar line and the object detected in the other camera was used to constrain correspondence. In addition, height and color were also used as features for tracking. The correspondences were obtained by combining these features using a Bayesian network. Dockstader and Tekalp[26] also employed Bayesian networks for tracking and occlusion reasoning across calibrated cameras with overlapping views. Sparse motion estimation and appearance were used as features. Mittal and Davis [84] used a region-based stereo algorithm to estimate the depth of points potentially lying on foreground objects and projected them on the ground plane. The objects were located by examining the clusters of the projected points. Kang et al.[64] presented a method for tracking in stationary and pan-tilt-zoom cameras. The ground planes in the moving and stationary cameras were registered. The moving camera sequences were stabilized by using affine transformations. The location of each object was then projected into a global coordinate frame for tracking. The object appearance was modeled by partitioning the object region into its polar representation. In each partition a Gaussian distribution modeled the color variation.

Lee et al. [71] proposed an approach for tracking in cameras with overlapping FOV's that did not require explicit calibration. The camera calibration information was recovered by matching motion trajectories obtained from different views and plane homographies were computed from the most frequent matches. Khan et al. [68] avoided explicit calibration by using the field of view (FOV) line constraints to handoff labels from one camera to another. The FOV information was learned during a training phase. Using this information, when an object was viewed in one camera, all the other cameras in which the object was visible could be predicted. Tracking in individual cameras was needed to be resolved before handoff could occur.

Most of the above mentioned tracking methods require a large overlap in the FOVs of the cameras. This requirement is usually prohibitive in terms of cost and computational resources for surveillance of wide areas.

5.2.2 Multi-Camera Tracking Methods for Non-Overlapping Views:

To track people in an environment not fully covered by the camera fields of view, Collins et al. [19] developed a system consisting of multiple calibrated cameras and a site model. Normalized cross correlation of detected objects and their location on the 3D site model were used for tracking . Huang and Russel [47] presented a probabilistic approach for tracking vehicles across two cameras on a highway. The solution presented was application specific, i.e., assumption of vehicles travelling in one direction, vehicles being in one of three lanes, and solution formulation for only two calibrated cameras. The appearance was modeled by the mean of the color of the whole object, which is not enough to distinguish between multi-colored objects like people. Transition times were modeled as Gaussian distributions and the initial transition probabilities were assumed to be known. The problem was transformed into a weighted assignment problem for establishing correspondence. Huang and Russel also provided an online version of their correspondence algorithm. The online algorithm trades off correct correspondence accuracy with solution space coverage, which forced them to commit early and possibly make erroneous correspondences. Kettnaker and Zabih [66] used a Bayesian formulation of the problem of reconstructing the paths of objects across multiple cameras. Their system required manual input of the topology of allowable paths of movement and the transition probabilities. The appearances of objects were represented by using histograms. In Kettnaker and Zabih's formulation, the positions, velocities and transition times of objects across cameras were not jointly modeled. However, this assumption does not hold in practice as these features are usually highly correlated.

Ellis et al. [80] determined the topology of a camera network by using a two stage algorithm. First the entry and exit zones of each camera were determined, then the links between these zones across cameras were found using the co-occurrence of entry and exit events. The proposed method assumes that correct correspondences will cluster in the feature space (location and time) while the wrong correspondences will generally be scattered across the feature space. The basic assumption is that if an entry and exit at a certain time interval are more likely than a random chance then they should have a higher likelihood of being linked. Recently, Stauffer [114] proposed an improved linking method which tested the hypothesis that the correlation between exit and entry events that may or may not contain valid object transitions is similar to the expected correlation when there are no valid transitions. This allowed the algorithm (unlike [80]) to handle the case where exit-entrance events may be correlated, but the correlation is not due to valid object transitions. Rahimi et al. [99] proposed a method to reconstruct the complete path of an object as it moved in a scene observed by non-overlapping cameras and to recover the ground plane calibration of the cameras. They modeled the dynamics of the moving object as a Markovian process. Given the location and velocity of the object from the multiple cameras, they estimated the trajectory most compatible with the object dynamics using a non-linear minimization scheme. The authors assumed that the objects moved on a ground plane and that all trajectory data of the object was available. Therefore, the proposed approach was not suitable for an online implementation.

Porikli [98] proposed a method to match object appearances over non-overlapping cameras. In his approach, a brightness transfer function (BTF) is computed for every pair of cameras, such that the BTF maps an observed color value in one camera to the corresponding observation in the other camera. Once such a mapping is known, the correspondence problem is reduced to the matching of transformed histograms or appearance models. However, this mapping, i.e., the BTF varies from frame to frame depending on a large number of parameters that include illumination, scene geometry, exposure time, focal length, and aperture size of each camera. Thus a single pre-computed BTF can not usually be used to match objects for moderately long sequences. Recently, Shan et al. [111] presented an unsupervised approach to learn edge measures for appearance matching between non-overlapping views. The matching was performed by computing the probability of two observations from two cameras being generated by the same or different object. Gaussian pdfs were used to compute the same/different probabilities. The proposed solution required the edge images of vehicles to be registered together. Note that the requirement for registering object images might not be possible for non-rigid objects like pedestrians. Moreover, this requirement also constrains the views of the objects in the different cameras to be somewhat similar.

In the next section we present a probabilistic formulation of the multi-camera tracking problem.

5.3 Formulation of the Multi-Camera Tracking Problem

Suppose that we have a system of r cameras $C_1, C_2, \ldots, C_r$ with non-overlapping views. Further, assume that there are n objects $p_1, p_2, \ldots, p_n$ in the environment (the number of the objects is not assumed to be known). Each of these objects is viewed from different cameras at different time instants. Assume that the task of single camera tracking is already solved, and let $\mathbf{O}$ be the set of all observations. Moreover, let $O_j = \{O_{j,1}, O_{j,2}, \ldots, O_{j,m_j}\}$ be the set of m_j observations that were observed by the camera C_j. Each observation $O_{j,a}$ is generated by an object in the field of view of camera C_j. The observations consist of two features, appearance of the object $O_{j,a}(app)$ and space-time features of the object $O_{j,a}(st)$ (location, velocity, time etc.). It is reasonable to assume that both $O_{j,a}(app)$ and $O_{j,a}(st)$ are independent of each other. The problem of multi-camera tracking is to find which of the observations in the system of cameras belong to the same object. It is helpful to view the set of observations of each object as a chain of observations with earlier observations preceding the latter ones. The task of grouping the observations of each object can then be seen as linking the consecutive observations in each such chain. Since we have assumed that the single camera tracking problem is solved, the multi-camera tracking task is to link the observations of an object exiting one camera to its observations entering another camera, as the object moves through the system of cameras.

For a formal definition of the problem, let a hypothesized correspondence between two consecutive observations, i.e., exit from one camera and entrance into another, $O_{i,a}$ and $O_{j,b}$ respectively, be denoted as $k_{i,a}^{j,b}$. Moreover, Let $\phi_{k_{i,a}^{j,b}}$ be a binary random variable which is true if and only if $k_{i,a}^{j,b}$ is a valid hypothesis, i.e., $O_{i,a}$ and $O_{j,b}$ are consecutive observations of the same object. We need to find a set of correspondences $K = \{k_{i,a}^{j,b}, \ldots\}$ such that $k_{i,a}^{j,b} \in K$ if and only if $\phi_{k_{i,a}^{j,b}}$ is true.

Let Σ be the solution space of the multi-camera tracking problem. From the above discussion, we know that each observation of an object is preceded or succeeded by a maximum of one observation (of the same object). Hence, if K is a candidate solution in Σ, then for all $\left\{ k_{i,a}^{j,b}, k_{p,c}^{r,e} \right\} \subseteq K$, $(i,a) \neq (p,c) \wedge (j,b) \neq (r,e)$. In addition, let Φ_K be a random variable which is true if and only if K represents a valid set of correspondences, i.e., all correspondences are correctly established. We want to find a feasible solution in the space Σ of all feasible solutions that maximizes the likelihood, i.e.,

$$K' = \arg\max_{K \in \Sigma} P\left(\mathbf{O} | \Phi_K = true \right).$$

Assuming that each correspondence, i.e., a matching between two observations, is conditionally independent of other observations and correspondences, we have:

$$P\left(\mathbf{O} | \Phi_K = true \right) = \prod_{k_{i,a}^{j,b} \in K} P\left(O_{i,a}, O_{j,b} | \phi_{k_{i,a}^{j,b}} = true \right). \tag{5.1}$$

Using the above equation along with the independence of observations $O_{j,a}(app)$ and $O_{j,a}(st)$, for all a and j, we have,

$$P\left(\mathbf{O} | \Phi_K = true \right) = \prod_{k_{i,a}^{j,b} \in K} \left(P\left(O_{i,a}(app), O_{j,b}(app) | \phi_{k_{i,a}^{j,b}} = true \right) \right.$$
$$\left. P\left(O_{i,a}(st), O_{j,b}(st) | \phi_{k_{i,a}^{j,b}} = true \right) \right). \tag{5.2}$$

Thus the following term gives us the solution:

$$K' = \arg\max_{K \in \Sigma} \prod_{k_{i,a}^{j,b} \in K} \left(P\left(O_{i,a}(app), O_{j,b}(app) | \phi_{k_{i,a}^{j,b}} = true \right) \right.$$
$$\left. P\left(O_{i,a}(st), O_{j,b}(st) | \phi_{k_{i,a}^{j,b}} = true \right) \right)$$

This is equivalent to maximizing the following term,

$$K' = \arg\max_{K \in \Sigma} \sum_{k_{i,a}^{j,b} \in K} \log \left(P\left(O_{i,a}(app), O_{j,b}(app) | \phi_{k_{i,a}^{j,b}} = true \right) \right.$$
$$\left. P\left(O_{i,a}(st), O_{j,b}(st) | \phi_{k_{i,a}^{j,b}} = true \right) \right). \tag{5.3}$$

In order to obtain the ML estimate we need to know the space-time and appearance probability density functions. This issue is discussed in the next two sections.

5.4 Learning Inter-Camera Space-Time Probabilities

Learning is carried out by assuming that the correspondences are known . One way to achieve this is to use only appearance matching for establishing correspondence since space-time relationships between cameras are unknown. Note that during training it is not necessary to correspond all objects across cameras. Only the best matches can be used for learning.

Suppose we have a sample S consisting of n, d dimensional, data points $x_1, x_2, \ldots, x_n$ from a multi-variate distribution $p(\mathbf{x})$. If the data is continuous, then the Parzen windows technique [27, 126] can be used to estimate its density . In our case, the position/time feature vector $\mathbf{x}$, used for learning the space-time pdfs from camera C_i to C_j, i.e., $P\left(O_{i,a}(sp), O_{j,b}(sp) | \phi_{k_{i,a}^{j,b}=true}\right)$, is a vector, consisting of the exit and entry locations in cameras, indices of entry and exit cameras, exit velocities, and the time interval between exit and entry events. The camera indices are treated as discrete features while the rest of the vector components are treated as continuous data. Since we have a mixed, i.e. continuous and discrete, data Parzen windows cannot be used directly to estimate the pdf. We have used a mixed density estimator proposed by Li and Racin [74] to obtain the space-time pdf. Let $\mathbf{x} = (\mathbf{x}', \mathbf{x}'')$, where $\mathbf{x}'$ is a d' dimensional vector representing the continuous components of $\mathbf{x}$. $\mathbf{x}''$ is a d'' dimensional vector representing the discrete components and $d = d' + d''$. In addition, Let x_t'' be the tth component of $\mathbf{x}''$ and suppose that x_t'' can assume $c_t \geq 2$ different values, where $(t = 1, 2 \ldots d'')$. The mixed density estimator is defined as

$$\hat{p}(\mathbf{x}) = \frac{1}{n} |\mathbf{H}|^{-\frac{1}{2}} \sum_{i=1}^{n} \kappa(\mathbf{H}^{-\frac{1}{2}}(\mathbf{x}' - \mathbf{x}_i')) \psi(\mathbf{x}'', \mathbf{x}_i'', \zeta), \qquad (5.4)$$

where the d' variate kernel $\kappa(\mathbf{x}')$, for continuous components, is a bounded function satisfying $\int \kappa(\mathbf{x}')d\mathbf{x}' = 1$, and $\mathbf{H}$ is the symmetric $d' \times d'$ bandwidth matrix. ψ is a multivariate kernel function for discrete components, defined as

$$\psi(\mathbf{x}'', \mathbf{x}_i'', \zeta) = c_0(1 - \zeta)^{d'' - dif_{i,x}}(\zeta)^{dif_{i,x}} \qquad (5.5)$$

where $dif_{i,x} = d'' - \sum_{t=1}^{d''} \ell(x_t'' - x_{i,t}'')$, and ℓ is the indicator function, ζ is the scalar discrete bandwidth parameter, and $c_0 = \Pi_{t=1..d''} \frac{1}{c_t - 1}$ is a normalization constant.

The multivariate kernel $\kappa(\mathbf{x}')$ can be generated from a product of symmetric univariate kernels κ_u, i.e., $\kappa(\mathbf{x}') = \Pi_{j=1}^{d'} \kappa_u(x_j')$. We use univariate Gaussian kernels to generate $\kappa(\mathbf{x}')$. Moreover, to reduce the complexity, $\mathbf{H}$ is assumed to be a diagonal matrix, i.e., $\mathbf{H} = diag[h_1^2, h_2^2, \ldots, h_{d'}^2]$, and the smoothing parameter for discrete variables ζ is chosen to be the same for both discrete components. The value of ζ is chosen to extremely small (approaching zero) because we do not want transitions across a pair of cameras being smoothed over and affecting transition probabilities between other cameras.

Each time, a correspondence is made during the training phase, the observed feature is added to the sample S. The observations of an object exiting from one camera and entering into another are separated by a certain time interval. We refer to this interval as *inter-camera travel time*. Following are some key observations that are modeled by the proposed system.

- The dependence of the inter-camera travel time on the magnitude and direction of motion of the object.
- The dependence of the inter-camera travel time interval on the location of exit from one camera and location of entrance in the other.
- The correlation among the locations of exits and entrances in cameras.

Since the correspondences are known in the training phase, the likely time intervals and exit/entrance locations are learned by estimating the pdf. The reason for using the kernel density estimation approach is that, rather than imposing assumptions, the nonparametric technique allows us to directly approximate the d dimensional density describing the joint pdf. It is also guaranteed to converge to any density function with enough training samples [27]. Moreover, it does not impose any restrictions on the shape of the function, neither does it assume independence between the feature set.

5.5 Estimating Change in Appearances across Cameras

In addition to the space-time information, we want to model the changes in the appearance of an object from one camera to another . The idea here is to learn the change in the color of objects, as they move between the cameras, from the training data and use this as a cue for establishing correspondences. One possible way of doing this was proposed by Porikli [98]. In his approach, a brightness transfer function (BTF) f_{ij} is computed for every pair of cameras C_i and C_j, such that f_{ij} maps an observed brightness value in Camera C_i to the corresponding observation in Camera C_j . Once such a mapping is known, the correspondence problem is reduced to the matching of transformed histograms or appearance models. Note that a necessary condition, for the existence of a one-to-one mapping of brightness values from one camera to another, is that the objects are planar and only have diffuse reflectance. Moreover, this mapping is not unique and it varies from frame to frame depending on a large number of parameters that include illumination, scene geometry, exposure time, focal length, and aperture size of each camera. Thus a single pre-computed mapping can not usually be used to match objects for any moderately long sequence.

In the following subsections, we show that despite a large number of unknown parameters, all BTFs from a given camera to another camera lie in a low dimensional subspace. Moreover, we present a method to learn this subspace from the training data and use this information to determine how likely it is for observations in different cameras to belong to the same object. In other words, given observations

$O_{i,a}(app)$ and $O_{j,b}(app)$ from cameras C_i and C_j respectively, and given all possible brightness transfer functions from camera C_i to camera C_j, we want to estimate the probability that the observations $O_{i,a}(app)$ and $O_{j,b}(app)$ belong to the same object.

5.5.1 The Space of Brightness Transfer Functions

Let $L_i(p,t)$ denote the scene reflectance at a (world) point p of an object that is illuminated by white light, when viewed from camera C_i at time instant t. By the assumption that the objects do not have specular reflectance, we may write $L_i(p,t)$ as a product of (a) material related terms, $M_i(p,t) = M(p)$ (for example, albedo) and (b) illumination/camera geometry and object shape related terms, $G_i(p,t)$, i.e.,

$$L_i(p,t) = M(p)G_i(p,t). \tag{5.6}$$

The above given model is valid for commonly used Bi-directional Reflectance Distribution Function (BRDF) , such as, the Lambertian model and the generalized Lambertian model [91] (See Table 5.1). By the assumption of planarity, $G_i(p,t) = G_i(q,t) = G_i(t)$, for all points p and q on a given object. Hence, we may write, $L_i(p,t) = M(p)G_i(t)$. The image irradiance $E_i(p,t)$ is proportional to

Table 5.1 Commonly used BRDF models that satisfy Equation 5.6. The subscripts i and r denote the incident and the reflected directions measured with respect to surface normal. I is the source intensity, ρ is the albedo, σ is the surface roughness, $\alpha = \max(\theta_i, \theta_r)$ and $\beta = \min(\theta_i, \theta_r)$. Note that for generalized Lambertian model to satisfy Equation 5.6, we must assume that the surface roughness σ is constant over the plane.

Model	M	G
Lambertian	ρ	$\frac{I}{\pi}\cos\theta_i$
Generalized Lambertian	ρ	$\frac{I}{\pi}\cos\theta_i \left[1 - \frac{0.5\sigma^2}{\sigma^2+0.33} + \frac{0.15\sigma^2}{\sigma^2+0.09}\cos(\phi_i - \phi_r)\sin\alpha\tan\beta\right]$

the scene radiance $L_i(p,t)$ [45], and is given as:

$$E_i(p,t) = L_i(p,t)Y_i(t) = M(p)G_i(t)Y_i(t), \tag{5.7}$$

where $Y_i(t) = \frac{\pi}{4}\left(\frac{d_i(t)}{h_i(t)}\right)^2 \cos^4\alpha_i(p,t) = \frac{\pi}{4}\left(\frac{d_i(t)}{h_i(t)}\right)^2 c$, is a function of camera parameters at time t. $h_i(t)$ and $d_i(t)$ are the focal length and diameter (aperture) of lens respectively, and $\alpha_i(p,t)$ is the angle that the principal ray from point p makes with the optical axis. The fall off in sensitivity due to the term $\cos^4\alpha_i(p,t)$ over an object is considered negligible [45] and may be replaced with a constant c.

If $X_i(t)$ is the time of exposure, and g_i is the radiometric response function of the camera C_i, then the measured (image) brightness of point p, $B_i(p,t)$, is related to the image irradiance as

$$B_i(p,t) = g_i\left(E_i(p,t)X_i(t)\right) = g_i\left(M(p)G_i(t)Y_i(t)X_i(t)\right), \qquad (5.8)$$

i.e., the brightness, $B_i(p,t)$, of the image of a world point p at time instant t, is a nonlinear function of the product of its material properties $M(p)$, geometric properties $G_i(t)$, camera parameters, $Y_i(t)$ and $X_i(t)$. Consider two cameras, C_i and C_j, assume that a world point p is viewed by cameras C_i and C_j at time instants t_i and t_j respectively. Since material properties M of a world point remain constant, we have,

$$M(p) = \frac{g_i^{-1}\left(B_i(p,t_i)\right)}{G_i(t_i)Y_i(t_i)X_i(t_i)} = \frac{g_j^{-1}\left(B_j(p,t_j)\right)}{G_j(t_j)Y_j(t_j)X_j(t_j)}. \qquad (5.9)$$

Hence, the brightness transfer function from the image of camera C_i at time t_i to the image of camera C_j at time t_j is given by:

$$B_j(p,t_j) = g_j\left(\frac{G_j(t_j)Y_j(t_j)X_j(t_j)}{G_i(t_i)Y_i(t_i)X_i(t_i)}g_i^{-1}\left(B_i(p,t_i)\right)\right) = g_j\left(w(t_i,t_j)g_i^{-1}\left(B_i(p,t_i)\right)\right), \qquad (5.10)$$

where $w(t_i,t_j)$ is a function of camera parameters and illumination/scene geometry of cameras C_i and C_j at time instants t_i and t_j respectively. Since Equation 5.10 is valid for any point p on the object visible in the two cameras, we may drop the argument p from the notation. Also, since it is implicit in the discussion that the BTF is different for any two pair of frames, we will also drop the arguments t_i and t_j for the sake of simplicity. Let f_{ij} denote a BTF from camera C_i to camera C_j, then,

$$B_j = g_j\left(wg_i^{-1}(B_i)\right) = f_{ij}(B_i). \qquad (5.11)$$

We use a non-parametric form of the BTF by sampling f_{ij} at a set of fixed increasing brightness values $B_i(1) < B_i(2) < \ldots < B_i(n)$, and representing it as a vector. That is, $(B_j(1),\ldots,B_j(n))=(f_{ij}(B_i(1)),\ldots,f_{ij}(B_i(n)))$. We denote the space of brightness transfer functions (SBTF) from camera C_i to camera C_j by Γ_{ij}. It is easy to see that the dimension of Γ_{ij} can be at most d_{max}, where d_{max} is the number of discrete brightness values (For most imaging systems, $d_{max} = 256$). However, the following theorem shows that BTFs actually lie in a small subspace of the d_{max} dimensional space.

Theorem 1

The subspace of brightness transfer functions Γ_{ij} has dimension at most m if for all $a,x \in \mathbf{R}$, $g_j(ax) = \sum_{u=1}^{m} r_u(a)s_u(x)$, where g_j is the radiometric response function of camera C_j, and for all u, $1 \leq u \leq m$, r_u and s_u are arbitrary but fixed 1D functions.

Proof of Theorem 1 Let g_i and g_j be the radiometric response functions of cameras C_i and C_j respectively. Also assume that for all $a,x \in \mathbf{R}$, $g_j(ax) = \sum_{u=1}^{m} r_u(a)s_u(x)$, where r_u and s_u are some arbitrary (but fixed) 1D functions, $1 \leq u \leq m$. Let f_{ij} be a brightness transfer function from camera C_i to camera C_j, then according to Equation 5.11, f_{ij} is given as:

$$f_{ij} = g_j\left(wg_i^{-1}(\mathbf{B}_i)\right) = \left[g_j\left(wg_i^{-1}(B_i(1))\right)\ g_j\left(wg_i^{-1}(B_i(2))\right)\ldots g_j\left(wg_i^{-1}(B_i(n))\right)\right]^T$$

Since $g_j(ax) = \sum_{u=1}^{m} r_u(a)s_u(x)$, we may write f_{ij} as follows:

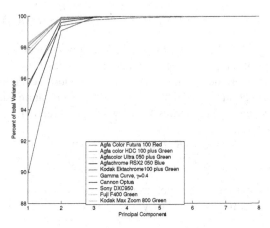

Fig. 5.2 Plots of the percentage of total variance accounted by m principal components (x-axis) of the subspace of brightness transfer functions from synthetic camera C_1 to camera C_i. Note that each synthetic camera was assigned a radiometric response function of a real world camera/film and a collection of BTFs was generated between pairs of synthetic cameras by varying w in the equation 5.11. PCA was performed on this collection of BTFs. The plot confirms that a very hight percentage of total variance is accounted by first 3 or 4 principal components of the subspace.

$$f_{ij} = \sum_{u=1}^{m} r_u(w) \left[s_u \left(g_i^{-1} \left(B_i(1) \right) \right) \ s_u \left(g_i^{-1} \left(B_i(2) \right) \right) \ldots \ s_u \left(g_i^{-1} \left(B_i(n) \right) \right) \right]^T$$
$$= \sum_{u=1}^{m} r_u(w) s_u \left(g_i^{-1} (\mathbf{B}_i) \right)$$

Thus, each brightness transfer function $f_{ij} \in \Gamma_{ij}$ can be represented as a linear combination of m vectors, $s_u \left(g_i^{-1} (\mathbf{B}_i) \right)$, $1 \leq u \leq m$. Hence, the dimension of space Γ_{ij} is at most m.

From Theorem 1, we see that the upper bound on the dimension of subspace depends on the radiometric response function of camera C_j. Though, the radiometric response functions are usually nonlinear and differ from one camera to another. They do not have exotic forms and are well-approximated by simple parametric models. Many authors have approximated the radiometric response function of a camera by a gamma function [32, 81], i.e., $g(x) = \lambda x^\gamma + \mu$. Then, for all $a, x \in \mathbf{R}$,

$$g(ax) = \lambda (ax)^\gamma + \mu = \lambda a^\gamma x^\gamma + \mu = r_1(a) s_1(x) + r_2(a) s_2(x),$$

where, $r_1(a) = a^\gamma$, $s_1(x) = \lambda x^\gamma$, $r_2(a) = 1$, and $s_2(x) = \mu$. Hence, by Theorem 1, if the radiometric response function of camera C_j is a gamma function, then the SBTF Γ_{ij} has dimensions at most 2. As compared to gamma functions, polynomials are a more general approximation of the radiometric response function. Once again, for a degree q polynomial $g(x) = \sum_{u=0}^{q} \lambda_u x^u$ and for any $a, x \in R$, we can write $g(ax) = \sum_{u=0}^{q} r_u(a) s_u(x)$ by putting $r_u(a) = a^u$ and $s_u(x) = \lambda_u x^u$, for all $0 \leq u \leq q$. Thus, the dimension of the SBTF Γ_{ij} is bounded by one plus the degree of the polynomial that approximates g_j. It is stated in [40] that most of the real world response functions are sufficiently well approximated by a low degree polynomial, e.g., a polynomial of degree less than or equal to 10. Thus, given our assumptions, the space of inter-camera BTFs will also be a polynomial of degree less than or equal to 10.

In Fig 5.2, we show empirically that the assertions made in this subsection remain valid for real world radiometric response functions. In the next subsection, we will give a method for estimating the BTFs and their subspace from training data in a multi-camera tracking scenario.

5.5.2 Estimation of Inter-Camera BTFs and their Subspace

Consider a pair of cameras C_i and C_j. Corresponding observations of an object across this camera pair can be used to compute an inter-camera BTF . One way to determine this BTF is to estimate the pixel to pixel correspondence between the object views in the two cameras (see Equation 5.11). However, self occlusion, change of scale and geometry, and different object poses can make finding pixel to pixel correspondences from views of the same object in two different cameras impossible. Thus, we employ normalized histograms of object brightness values for the BTF computation. Such histograms are relatively robust to changes in object pose [117]. In order to compute the BTF, we assume that the percentage of image points on the observed object $O_{i,a}(app)$ with brightness less than or equal to B_i is equal to the percentage of image points in the observation $O_{j,b}(app)$ with brightness less than or equal to B_j. Note that, a similar strategy was adopted by Grossberg and Nayar [39] to obtain a BTF between images taken from the same camera of the same view but in different illumination conditions. Now, if H_i and H_j are the normalized cumulative histograms of object observations I_i and I_j respectively, then $H_i(B_i) = H_j(B_j) = H_j(f_{ij}(B_i))$. Therefore, we have

$$f_{ij}(B_i) = H_j^{-1}(H_i(B_i)), \tag{5.12}$$

where H^{-1} is the inverted cumulative histogram.

As discussed in the previous sub-section, the BTF between two cameras changes with time due to illumination conditions, camera parameters, etc. We use Equation 5.12 to estimate the brightness transfer function $\mathbf{f_{ij}}$ for every pair of observations in the training set. Let F_{ij} be the collection of all the brightness transfer functions obtained in this manner, i.e., $\{\mathbf{f}_{(ij)n}\}, n \in \{1,\ldots,N\}$. To learn the subspace of this collection we use the probabilistic Principal Component Analysis PPCA [120]. According to this model a d_{max} dimensional BTF $\mathbf{f_{ij}}$ can be written as

$$\mathbf{f_{ij}} = \mathbf{W}\mathbf{y} + \overline{\mathbf{f_{ij}}} + \varepsilon. \tag{5.13}$$

Here $\mathbf{y}$ is a normally distributed q dimensional latent (subspace) variable, $q < d_{max}$, $\mathbf{W}$ is a $d_{max} \times q$ dimensional projection matrix that relates the subspace variables to the observed BTF, $\overline{\mathbf{f_{ij}}}$ is the mean of the collection of BTFs, and ε is isotropic Gaussian noise, i.e., $\varepsilon \sim N(0, \sigma^2 \mathbf{I})$. Given that $\mathbf{y}$ and ε are normally distributed, the distribution of f_{ij} is given as

$$\mathbf{f_{ij}} \sim \mathcal{N}(\overline{\mathbf{f_{ij}}}, \mathbf{Z}), \tag{5.14}$$

where $\mathbf{Z} = \mathbf{WW}^T + \sigma^2 \mathbf{I}$. Now, as suggested in [120], the projection matrix $\mathbf{W}$ is estimated as

$$\mathbf{W} = \mathbf{U}_q (\mathbf{E}_q - \sigma^2 \mathbf{I})^{1/2} \mathbf{R}, \tag{5.15}$$

where the q column vectors in the $d_{max} \times q$ dimensional $\mathbf{U}_q$ are the eigenvectors of the sample covariance matrix of $\mathbf{F}_{ij}$, $\mathbf{E}_q$ is a $q \times q$ diagonal matrix of corresponding eigenvalues $\lambda_1, \ldots, \lambda_q$, and $\mathbf{R}$ is an arbitrary orthogonal rotation matrix which can be set to an identity matrix for computational purposes. The value of σ^2, which is the variance of the information 'lost' in the projection, is calculated as

$$\sigma^2 = \frac{1}{d_{max} - q} \sum_{v=q+1}^{d_{max}} \lambda_v. \tag{5.16}$$

Once the values of σ^2 and $\mathbf{W}$ are known, we can compute the probability of a particular BTF belonging to the learned subspace of BTFs by using the distribution in Equation 5.14.

Note that till now we have been dealing with only the brightness values of images and computing the brightness transfer functions. To deal with color images we treat each channel, i.e., R, G and B separately. The transfer function for each color channel is computed exactly as discussed above. The subspace parameters $\mathbf{W}$ and σ^2 are also computed separately for each color channel. Also note that we do not assume the knowledge of any camera parameters and response functions for the computation of these transfer functions and their subspace.

5.5.3 Computing Object Color Similarity Across Cameras Using the BTF Subspace

The observed color of an object can vary widely across multiple non-overlapping cameras due to change in scene illumination or any of the different camera parameters like gain and focal length. Note that, the training phase provides us the subspace of color transfer functions between the cameras, which models how colors of an object can change across the cameras. During the test phase, if the mapping between the colors of two observations is well explained by the learned subspace then it is likely that these observations are generated by the same object. Specifically, for two observations $O_{i,a}$ and $O_{j,b}$ with color transfer functions (whose distribution is given by Equation 5.14) $\mathbf{f}_{i,j}^{R}, \mathbf{f}_{i,j}^{G}$ and $\mathbf{f}_{i,j}^{B}$, we define the probability of the observations belonging to same object as

$$P_{i,j}(O_{i,a}(app), O_{j,b}(app)|k_{i,a}^{j,b}) = \prod_{ch \in \{R,G,B\}} \frac{1}{(2\pi)^{\frac{d}{2}} \left|\mathbf{Z}^{ch}\right|^{\frac{1}{2}}} e^{-\frac{1}{2}\left(\mathbf{f}_{ij}^{ch} - \overline{\mathbf{f}_{ij}^{ch}}\right)^{T}(\mathbf{Z}^{ch})^{-1}\left(\mathbf{f}_{ij}^{ch} - \overline{\mathbf{f}_{ij}^{ch}}\right)}, \quad (5.17)$$

where $\mathbf{Z} = \mathbf{W}\mathbf{W}^{T} + \sigma^{2}\mathbf{I}$. The ch superscript denotes the color channel for which the value of $\mathbf{Z}$ and $\overline{\mathbf{f}_{ij}}$ were calculated. For each color channel, the values of $\mathbf{W}$ and σ^{2} are computed from the training data using Equation 5.15 and Equation 5.16 respectively.

5.6 Establishing Correspondences

Recall from Section 5.3, that the problem of multi-camera tracking is to find a set of correspondences K', such that, each observation is preceded or succeeded by a maximum of one observation, and that maximizes the likelihood, i.e.,

$$K' = \arg\max_{K \in \Sigma} \sum_{k_{i,a}^{j,b} \in K} \log \left(P\left(O_{i,a}(app), O_{j,b}(app)|\phi_{k_{i,a}^{j,b}} = true\right) \right.$$
$$\left. P\left(O_{i,a}(st), O_{j,b}(st)|\phi_{k_{i,a}^{j,b}} = true\right) \right).$$

The problem of finding the ML solution can be modeled as a graph theoretical problem as follows : We construct a directed graph such that for each observation $O_{i,a}$, there is a corresponding vertex in the directed graph, while each hypothesized correspondence $k_{i,a}^{j,b}$ is modeled by an arc from the vertex of observation $O_{i,a}$ to the vertex of observation $O_{j,b}$. The weight of this arc of the hypothesized correspondence $k_{i,a}^{j,b}$ is computed from the space-time and appearance probability terms, in the summation in Equation 5.3. Note that these probabilities are computed using the methods described in Sections 5.4 and 5.5. With the constraint that an observation can correspond to at most one succeeding and one preceding observation, it is easy to see that each candidate solution is a set of directed paths (of length 0 or more) in this graph. Also, since each observation corresponds to a single object, each vertex of the graph must be in exactly one path of the solution. Hence, each candidate solution in the solution space is a set of directed paths in the constructed graph, such that each vertex of the graph is in exactly one path of this set. Such a set is called vertex disjoint path cover of a directed graph. The weight of a path cover is defined by the sum of all the weights of the edges in the path cover. Hence, a path cover with the maximum weight corresponds to the solution of the ML problem as defined in Equation 5.3.

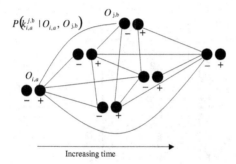

Increasing time

Fig. 5.3 An example of split graph (constructed from the directed graph) that formulates the multi-camera tracking problem. Each vertex of the directed graph is splitted into + (exit) and −(entry) vertices, such that the + vertex is adjacent to an edge for each arc going out of the vertex and the − vertex is adjacent to an edge for each arc coming into the vertex. The weight of an edge is the same as the weight of the corresponding arc. The graph is bipartite, since no + vertex is adjacent to a + vertex and no − vertex is adjacent to a − vertex.

The problem of finding a maximum weight path cover can be optimally solved in polynomial time if the directed graph is acyclic[110] . Recall that $k_{i,a}^{j,b}$ defines the hypothesis that the observations $O_{i,a}$ and $O_{j,b}$ are consecutive observations of the same object in the environment, with the observation $O_{i,a}$ preceding the observation $O_{j,b}$. Thus, by the construction of graph, all the arcs are in the direction of increasing time, and hence, the graph is acyclic. The maximum weight path cover of an acyclic directed graph can be found by reducing the problem to finding the maximum matching of an undirected bipartite graph. This bipartite graph is obtained by splitting every vertex v of the directed graph into two vertices v^- and v^+ such that each arc coming into the vertex v is substituted by an edge incident to the vertex v^-, while the vertex v^+ is connected to an edge for every arc going out of the vertex v in the directed graph (The bipartite graph obtained from the directed graph is shown in Figure 5.3). The edges in the maximum matching of the constructed bipartite graph correspond to the arcs in the maximum weight path cover of the original directed graph. The maximum matching of a bipartite graph can be found by an $O(n^{2.5})$ algorithm by Hopcroft and Karp [44], where n is the total number of vertices in graph G, i.e., the total number of observations in the system.

The method described above, assumes that the entire set of observations is available and hence cannot be used in real time applications. One approach to handle this type of problem in real time applications is to use a sliding window of a fixed time interval. This approach, however, involves a tradeoff between the quality of results and the timely availability of the output. In order to avoid making erroneous correspondences, we adaptively select the size of sliding window in the online version of our algorithm. This is achieved by examining the space-time pdfs for all observations (tracks) in the environment that are not currently visible in any of the cameras in the system and finding the time interval after which the probability of reappearance of all these observations in any camera is nearly zero. The size of sliding window is taken to be the size of this time interval, and the correspondences are established by selecting the maximum weight path cover of the graph within the window.

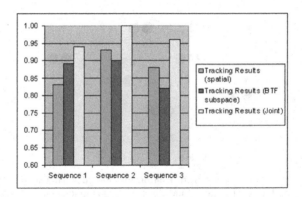

Fig. 5.4 Tracking Results. Tracking accuracy for each of the three sequences computed for three different cases. 1. by using only space-time model, 2. by using only appearance model, and 3. both models. The results improve greatly when both the space-time and appearance models are employed for establishing correspondence.

5.7 Results

In this section, we present the results of the proposed method in three different multi-camera scenarios. The scenarios differ from each other both in terms of camera topologies and scene illumination conditions, and include both indoor and outdoor settings. Each experiment consists of a supervised training phase and a testing phase. In both phases, the single camera object detection and tracking information is obtained by using the method proposed in [52]. In the training phase, the known correspondence information is used to compute the kernel density of the space-time features (entry and exit locations, exit velocity and inter-camera time interval) and the subspaces of transfer functions for each color channel (red, blue, and green). In the testing phase, these correspondences are computed using the proposed multi-camera correspondence algorithm. The performance of the algorithm is analyzed by comparing the resulting tracks to the ground truth. We say that an object in the scene is tracked *correctly* if it is assigned a single unique label for the complete duration of its presence in the area of interest. The *tracking accuracy* is defined as the ratio of the number of objects tracked correctly to the total number of objects that passed through the scene.

In order to determine the relative significance of each model and to show the importance of combining the space-time information with the appearance matching scheme, for each multi-camera scenario, the correspondences in the testing phase are computed for three different cases separately, by using i) only space-time model, ii) only appearance model, and iii) both models. The results of each of these cases are analyzed by using the above defined tracking accuracy as the evaluation measure. These results are summarized in Figure 5.4 and are explained below for each of the experimental setup.

The first experiment was conducted with two cameras, Camera 1 and Camera 2, in an outdoor setting. The camera topology is shown in Figure 5.5(a). The scene viewed by Camera 1 is a covered area under shade, whereas Camera 2 views an open area illuminated by the sunlight (please see Figure 5.7). It can be seen from the figure that there is a significant difference between the global illumination of the two scenes, and matching the appearances is considerably difficult without accurate modeling of the changes in appearance across the cameras. Training was performed by using a five minute sequence. The marginal of the space-time density for exit velocities from Camera 2 and the inter-camera travel time interval is shown in Figure 5.5(b). The marginal density shows a strong anti-correlation between the two space-time features and complies with the intuitive notion that for higher velocities there is a greater probability that the time interval will be less, whereas a

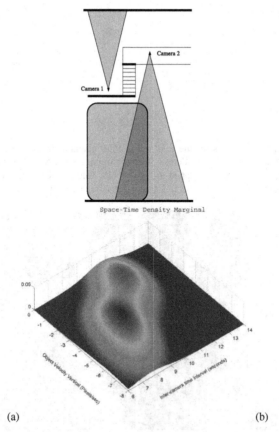

Fig. 5.5 (a) Two camera configuration for the first experiment. Field-of-view of each camera is shown with triangles. The cameras were mounted approximately 10 yards apart. It took 7 to 12 seconds for a person walking at normal speed to exit from the view of Camera 1 and enter Camera 2. The regions shown, that are not triangular, are the areas covered by grass; most people avoid walking over them. (b) The marginal of the inter-camera space-time density (learned from the training data) for exit velocities of objects from Camera 2 and the time taken by the objects to move from Camera 2 to Camera 1. Note if the object velocity is high a lesser inter-camera travel time is more likely, while for objects moving with lower velocities a longer inter-camera travel time is more likely.

longer time interval is likely for slower objects. In Figure 5.6 the transfer functions obtained from the first five correspondences from Camera 1 to Camera 2 are shown. Note that lower color values from Camera 1 are being mapped to higher color values in Camera 2 indicating that the same object is appearing much brighter in Camera 2 as compared to Camera 1.

The test phase consisted of a twelve minute long sequence. In this phase, a total of 68 tracks were recorded in the individual cameras and the algorithm detected 32 transitions across the cameras. Tracking accuracy for the test phase is shown in Figure 5.4.

Our second experimental setup consists of three cameras, Camera 1, Camera 2, and Camera 3, as shown in Figure 5.8(a). The field-of-view of each camera is also shown in the figure. It should be noted that there are several paths from one camera to the other, which make the sequence more complex. Training was done on a ten minute sequence in the presence of multiple persons. Fig-

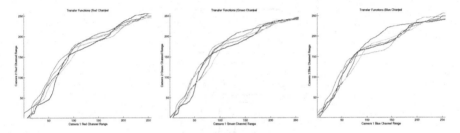

Fig. 5.6 The transfer functions for the R,G and B color channels from Camera 1 to Camera 2, obtained from the first five correspondences from the training data. Note that mostly lower color values from Camera 1 are being mapped to higher color values in Camera 2 indicating that the same object is appearing much brighter in Camera 2 as compared to Camera 1.

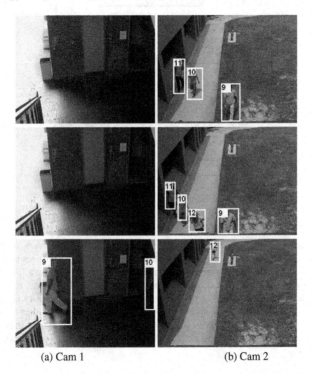

(a) Cam 1   (b) Cam 2

Fig. 5.7 Frames from sequence 1. Note that multiple persons are simultaneously exiting from camera 2 and entering at irregular intervals in camera 1. The first camera is overlooking a covered area while the second camera view is under direct sun light, therefore the observed color of objects is fairly different in the two views (also see Figure 5.12). Correct labels are assigned in this case due to accurate color modeling.

ure 5.8(b) shows the probabilities of entering Camera 2 from Camera 1, that were obtained during the training phase. Note that people like to take the shortest possible path between two points. This fact is clearly demonstrated by the space-time pdf, which shows a correlation between the y-coordinates of the entry and exit locations of the two cameras. That is, if an object exits Camera

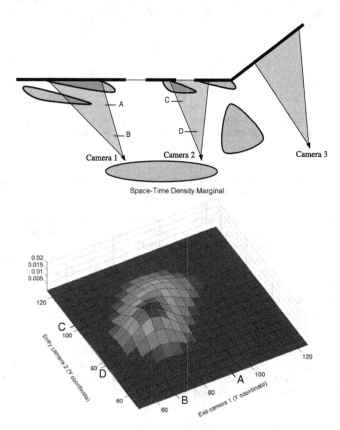

Fig. 5.8 (Top) Camera setup for sequence 2. Camera 2 and Camera 3 were mounted approximately 30 yards apart, while the distance between Camera 1 and Camera 2 was approximately 20 yards. It took 8 to 14 seconds for a person walking at normal speed to exit from the view of Camera 1 and enter Camera 2. The walking time between Camera 2 and 3 was between 10 to 18 seconds. The regions shown that are not triangular are patches of grass; most people avoid walking over them. The points A,B,C, and D are some regions where people exited and/or entered the camera field of view. (Bottom)The marginal of the inter-camera space-time density for exit location of objects from Camera 1 and Entry location in Camera 2. In the graph the *y* coordinates of right boundary of Camera 1 and left boundary of Camera 2 are plotted. Since most people walked in a straight path from Camera 1 to Camera 2 , i.e. from from point A to C and from point B to D as shown in (a), thus corresponding locations had a higher probability of being the exit/entry locations of the same person.

1 from point A, it is more probable that it will enter Camera 2 at point C rather than point D. The situation is reversed if the object exits Camera 1 from point B. Testing was carried out on a fifteen minute sequence. A total of 71 tracks in individual cameras were obtained and the algorithm detected 45 transitions within the cameras. The trajectories of the people moving through the scene in the testing phase are shown in Figure 5.9. Note that people did not stick to a narrow path between

Cam1   Cam2   Cam3

Fig. 5.9 Trajectories of people for the camera setup 2. Trajectories of the same person are shown in the same gray-level. There were a total of 27 people who walked through the environment.

Camera 1 and Camera 2, but this did not affect the tracking accuracy and all the correspondences were established correctly when both space-time and appearance models were used (see Figure 5.4). Figure 5.15 shows some tracking instances in this sequence. In the third experiment, three cameras Camera 1, Camera 2, and Camera 3 were used for an indoor/outdoor setup. Camera 1 was placed indoor while the other two cameras were placed outdoor. The placements of the cameras along with their fields of view are shown in Figure 5.10. Training was done on an eight minute sequence in the presence of multiple persons. Testing was carried out on a fifteen minute sequence. Figure 5.11 shows some tracking instances for the test sequence. The algorithm detected 49 transitions among the total of 99 individual tracks that were obtained during this sequence, out of which only two correspondences were incorrect. One such error was caused by a person staying, for a much longer than expected duration, in an unobserved region. That is, the person stood in an unobserved region for a long time and then entered another camera but the time constraint (due to the space-time model) forced the assignment of a new label to the person. Such a scenario could have been handled if there were similar examples in the training phase. The aggregate tracking results for the sequence are given in Figure 5.4. It is clear from Figure 5.4 that both the appearance and space-time models are important sources of information as the tracking results improve significantly when both the models are used jointly.

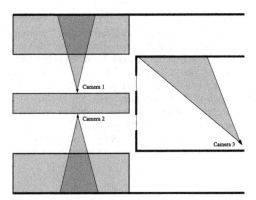

Fig. 5.10 Camera setup for sequence 3. It is an *Indoor/Outdoor Sequence*. Camera 3 is placed indoor while Cameras 1 and 2 are outdoor. The distance between camera 3 and the other two cameras is around 20 meters.

(a) Cam 3   (b) Cam 2   (c) Cam 1

Fig. 5.11 Frames from Sequence 3 test phase. A person is assigned a unique label as it moves through the camera views.

In Table 5.2, we show the number of principal components that account for 99% of the total variance in the inter-camera BTFs computed during the training phase. About 40 correspondences(supervised) were used for training for each camera pair between which there was a direct, i.e., without going through an intermediate camera view, movement of people. Even though the experimental setup does not follow the assumptions of Section 5.5, such as planarity of objects, the small number of principal components indicates that the inter-camera BTFs lie in a low dimension subspace even in more general conditions.

Table 5.2 The number of principal components that account for 99% of the variance in the BTFs. Note that for all camera pairs a maximum of 7 principal components were sufficient to account for the subspace of the BTFs.

Sequence #	Camera Pair	# of principal components (Red)	# of principal components (Green)	# of principal components (Blue)
1	1-2	6	5	5
2	1-2	7	7	7
2	2-3	7	7	6
3	1-3	7	6	7
3	2-3	7	7	7

In order to demonstrate the superiority of the subspace based method we compare it with the direct use of colors for tracking. For direct color base matching, instead of using Equation 5.17 for the computation of appearance probabilities $P_{i,j}(O_{i,a}(app), O_{j,b}(app)|k_{i,a}^{j,b})$, we define it in terms of the Bhattacharraya distance between the normalized histograms of the observations $O_{i,a}$ and $O_{i,b}$, i.e.,

$$P_{i,j}(O_{i,a}(app), O_{j,b}(app)|k_{i,a}^{j,b}) = \gamma e^{-\gamma D(h_i, h_j)}, \tag{5.18}$$

where h_i and h_j are the normalized histograms of the observations $O_{i,a}$ and $O_{j,b}$ and D is the modified Bhattacharraya distance [21] between two histograms and is given as

$$D(h_i, h_j) = \sqrt{1 - \sum_{v=1}^{m} \sqrt{\hat{h}_{i,v} \hat{h}_{j,v}}}, \qquad (5.19)$$

where m is the total number of bins. The Bhattacharraya coefficient ranges between zero and one and is a metric.

Once again, the tracking accuracy was computed for all three multi-camera scenarios using the color histogram based model (Equation 5.18). The comparison of the proposed appearance modeling approach with the direct color based appearance matching is presented in Figure 5.13, and clearly shows that the subspace based appearance model performs significantly better.

Table 5.3 The average normalized reconstruction errors for BTFs between observations of the same object and also between observation of different objects.

Sequence #	Average BTF Reconstruction Error (Correct Matches)	Average BTF Reconstruction Error (Incorrect Matches)
1	.0003	.0016
2	.0002	.0018
3	.0005	.0011

For further comparison of the two methods, we consider two observations, O_a and O_b, in the testing phase, with histograms $H(O_a)$ and $H(O_b)$ respectively. We first compute a BTF, $\mathbf{f}$, between the two observations and reconstruct the BTF, $\mathbf{f}^*$, from the subspace estimated from the training data, i.e., $\mathbf{f}^* = \mathbf{W}\mathbf{W}^T (\mathbf{f} - \bar{\mathbf{f}}) + \bar{\mathbf{f}}$. Here $\mathbf{W}$ is the projection matrix obtained in the training phase. The first observation O_a is then transformed using $\mathbf{f}^*$, and the histogram of the object O_b is matched with the histograms of both O_a and $\mathbf{f}^*(O_a)$ by using the Bhattacharraya distance. When both the observations O_a and O_b belong to the same object, the transformed histogram gives a much better match as compared to direct histogram matching, as shown in Figures 5.12 and 5.14. However, if the observations O_a and O_b belong to different objects then the BTF is reconstructed poorly, (since it does not lie in the subspace of valid BTFs), and the Bhattacharraya distance for the transformed observation either increases or does not change significantly. The normalized reconstruction error of the BTF, $\mathbf{f}^*$-Reconstruction Error$= \|\mathbf{f} - \mathbf{f}^*\| / \tau$, where τ is a normalizing constant, is also shown in the figures. The aggregate results for the reconstruction error, for the BTFs between the same object and also between different objects are given in Table 5.3. The above discussion suggests the applicability of the BTF subspace for the improvement of any multi-camera appearance matching scheme that uses color as one of its components.

Our multi-camera tracking system uses a client-server architecture, in which a client processor is associated with each camera. The advantage of this architecture is that the computationally expensive tasks of object detection and single camera tracking are performed at the client side, while the server only performs the multi-view correspondence. The communication between the client and server consists of histogram and trajectory information of objects, and this information is sent only when the objects exit or enter the field of view of a camera. Note that, the server does not use the images directly and thus the communication overhead is low. In our experiments, there was no significant difference in frame rates between the two camera and three camera setups. A near real time implementation, 5-10 frame/sec on 1.6 GHz machine, of the proposed multi-camera tracking approach was presented in a demo [55].

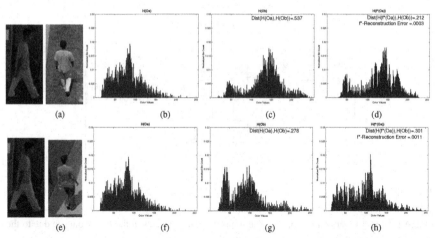

Fig. 5.12 (a) Observations O_a and O_b of the same object from camera 1 and camera 2 respectively from camera setup 1. (b) Histogram of observation O_a (All histograms are of the Red color channel). (c) Histogram of observation O_b. The Bhattacharraya distance between the two histograms of the same object is 0.537. (d) The Histogram of O_a after undergoing color transformation using the BTF reconstruction from the learned subspace. Note that after the transformation the histogram of $(f^*(O_a))$ looks fairly similar to the histogram of O_b. The Bhattacharraya distance reduces to 0.212 after the transformation. (e) Observation from camera 1 matched to an observation from a different object in camera 2. (f,g) Histograms of the observations. The distance between histograms of two different objects is 0.278 . Note that this is less than the distance between histograms of the same object. (h) Histogram after transforming the colors using the BTF reconstructed from the subspace. The Bhattacharraya distance increases to 0.301. Simple color matching gives a better match for the wrong correspondence. However, in the transformed space the correct correspondence gives the least bhattacharraya distance.

5.8 Conclusions

In this chapter, we propose an approach for tracking objects across multiple non-overlapping cameras. We show that accurate tracking is possible even when observations of the objects are not available for relatively long periods of time due to non-overlapping camera views. Furthermore we demonstrate that camera topology and inter-camera spatiotemporal relationships can be learned by observing motion of people as they move across the scene. In addition, it is also possible to learn the relationship between the appearance of objects across cameras by estimating the subspace of brightness transfer functions.

The spatio-temporal cues used to constrain correspondences include inter-camera time intervals, location of exit/entrances, and velocities of objects. Moreover, for appearance matching, a novel method of modeling the change of appearance across cameras is presented. We show that given some assumptions, all brightness transfer functions from a given camera to another camera lie in a low dimensional subspace. We also demonstrate empirically that even for real scenarios this

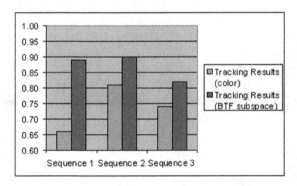

Fig. 5.13 Tracking accuracy: comparison of the BTF subspace based tracking method to simple color matching. A much improved matching is achieved in the transformed color space relative to direct color comparison of objects. The improvement is greater in the first sequence due to the large difference in the scene illumination in the two camera views.

subspace is low dimensional. The knowledge of camera parameters like focal length, aperture etc is not required for computation of the subspace of BTFs. The proposed system learns this subspace by using probabilistic principal component analysis on the BTFs obtained from the training data and uses it for the appearance matching. The space-time cues are combined with the appearance matching scheme in a ML framework for tracking. We have presented results on realistic scenarios to show the validity of the proposed approach.

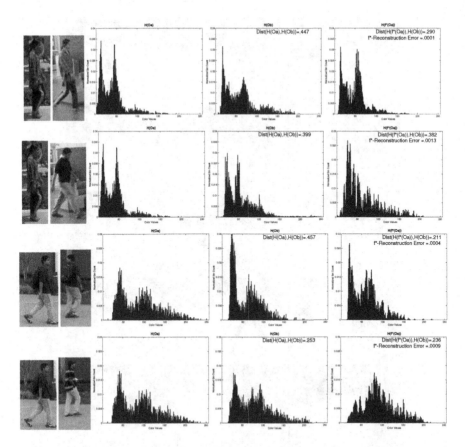

Fig. 5.14 Row 1: Observations from camera setup 3. The observations are of the same object from Camera 1 and Camera 2 respectively. Their blue channel histograms are also shown. The last histogram is obtained after transforming the colors with a reconstructed BTF f^* from the subspace. Note that the Bhattacharraya distance (shown at the top of the histograms) improves significantly after the transformation. Row 2: Observations of different objects and their blue channel histograms. Here there is no significant change in the Bhattacharraya distance after the transformation. Rows (3,4): Observations from camera setup 2. Here the direct use of color histograms results in a better match for the wrong correspondence. However after the color transformation, histograms of the same objects have the lesser Bhattacharraya distance between them.

(a) Camera 1   (b) Camera 2   (c) Camera 3

Fig. 5.15 consistent labelling for camera setup 2. Rows 1 and 2: people enter Camera 3. Row 3: A new person enters camera 2, note that he is given a previously unassigned label. Rows 4 to 8: People keep on moving across cameras. All persons retain unique labels.

Chapter 6

KNIGHT: SURVEILLANCE SYSTEM DEPLOYMENT

6.1 Introduction

The video analysis algorithms described in chapters 2 to 5 were integrated into the Knight multi-camera surveillance system. Knight is a fully automated surveillance and monitoring system that we developed at UCF Computer Vision Laboratory, and which is being used for projects funded by the Florida Department of Transportation (FDOT), Orlando Police Department, DARPA Small Business Technology Transfer (STTR) program, and Lockheed Martin Corporation. Knight is a *smart* Commercial Off the Shelf (COTS) surveillance system that detects, categorizes and tracks moving objects in the scene using state of the art computer vision techniques. It also flags significant events and presents a summary in terms of key frames and a textual description of observed activities to a human operator for final analysis and response decision.

Knight has been implemented in Visual C++. It is capable of running on both PCs and laptops. It operates at 10 to 15 Hz on a pentium 2.6 GHz machine with 512 MB RAM. It takes video input from any video camera capable of transmitting video through IEEE 1394 'firewire' cable. The system uses a client-server architecture . The single camera system, with an added network module, acts as a client. Each client transmits the track and appearance information of the objects, in its view, to the server. The server assigns global label to each object using the algorithm described in chapter 5 and maintains synchronization between information streams coming from the clients. The system uses the TCP/IP protocol for network communication and is capable of using both ethernet based and wireless networks.

6.2 Deploying Surveillance Systems: Ethical Considerations

The commonly stated reason for use of surveillance systems is to guard a country or a commercial enterprize against intrusion and attacks and, in general, to protect people from crime. As stated by George Orwell, "On the whole human beings want to be good, but not too good and not quite all the time". However, the impact of increased monitoring might go beyond the obvious domains of law enforcement and homeland security. Many contemporary thinkers, and most famously George Orwell [92] and Michel Foucault [33], have made a connection between the use of surveillance procedures and increased control and regulation by the state. The increasing deployment of Close Circuit Television Systems (CCTVs) have evoked privacy concerns by prominent civil rights groups like the American Civil Liberties Union (ACLU) [1].

O. Javed, M. Shah, *Automated Multi-Camera Surveillance: Algorithms and Practice*,
DOI: 10.1007/978-0-387-78881-4_6, © Springer Science+Business Media, LLC 2008

In spite of the potential of abuse, there are many benefits of the surveillance technology if the privacy concerns are adequately addressed. As written by N. Taylor [118],

> Though the allusion to Big Brother is a popular modern metaphor for the role of the State in social control, it ignores the numerous benefits increased surveillance has brought about. Surveillance does, undoubtedly, have two faces. It can act to curtail rights through, for example, reinforcing divisions within society, or it can be a vital tool in preventing and detecting crime. For citizens to accept and consent to certain forms of surveillance, that is to say its positive face, the state should be accountable for its actions.

The laws of the country will almost certainly change to cope with the proliferation of surveillance systems in everyday life. For a thorough treatment of the subject and to get versed with the current trends in the privacy vs. safety via surveillance debate, we refer the interested reader to the journal *Surveillance and Society* [2].

In our system, a far field of camera view is used and people or vehicle number plates are not identifiable. Moreover, no mechanism was used to determine the identity of the observed people. Thus we know where vehicles and people moved in the area under observation but there is no knowledge of *who* moved. During the actual deployment of system (after the initial experimental phase), no video data was stored rather only textual description or single images, in case of an alarm, were recorded by the system. In addition, the system was deployed in public areas with visible signs posted, warning that the area is under surveillance.

6.3 Knight in Action

Knight has been actively used in several surveillance related projects funded by different government and private agencies. For example, Knight is deployed for a project funded by FDOT to monitor the railroad grade crossings in order to prevent accidents involving trains and to automatically inform the authorities in case of any potential hazard, for example, the presence of a person or a vehicle on tracks while a train is approaching. There are approximately 261,000 highway-rail and pedestrian crossings in the United States according to the studies by the National Highway Traffic Safety Administration (NHTSA) and Federal Railroad Administration (FRA). According to the FRA's railroad safety report [3] , from 1998 to 2004, there were 21,952 highway-rail crossing incidents involving motor vehicles-averaging 3,136 incidents a year. In Florida alone, there were 650 highway-rail grade crossing incidents, resulting in 98 fatalities during this period. Thus, there is significant need for the exploration of the use of innovative technologies to monitor railroad grade crossings.

In addition to the the standard functionality of a surveillance system, the system deployed for FDOT allows the user to crop a zone (shown by a yellow bounding box in Figure 6.1) in the image corresponding to specific location in the scene. This zone (called danger zone) is usually the area in the scene of interest, where the presence of a person or vehicle can be hazardous in case a train is approaching. The system receives two inputs, one from the traffic signal (triggered when a train approaches) and the other from the detection module giving the position of pedestrians and vehicles with respect to the danger zone. A simple rule-based algorithm recognizes events based on the object location and trajectory patterns . At the onset of an undesirable event, such as presence of a person or a vehicle on or near tracks while a train is approaching, an audio alert is generated, and an email is sent to an authorized individual through a wireless network. The system also has the capability to detect the presence of a train in the video using the motion information in a designated area. We evaluated the performance of different modules of the system (detection, tracking and classification), by manually determining the ground truth from six hours of videos and comparing the ground truth to the results of the automated system. The Knight system was set up at

Fig. 6.1 Knight at Railroads: A danger zone is defined manually through a Graphical User Interface (GUI). An alarm is generated if People or vehicles (but not trains) enter the danger zone. The bounding box of an object outside the danger zone is displayed in white. The bounding box of an individual turns black as it enters the the danger zone.

two different highway-railroad crossings in Central Florida and a total of five videos were collected from different views and in different conditions, e.g., time of day, lighting, wind, camera focus, traffic density e.t.c. The collection of videos under different weather conditions, such as sunny, overcast, and partly cloudy weather ensured that the system was tested under different as well as constantly changing illumination conditions. Note that the system only works in day-time and turns off automatically when the illumination is below certain predefined level, hence the testing was only performed during day-time. In addition, the system also does not perform during rain and storms and these weather conditions were not considered during testing. The Knight system was used to detect, track, and classify the moving objects in the collected videos. The accuracy of object detection was measured as the ratio of the number of correct detections and the total number of objects. The system correctly detected 706 objects out of 725 and it generated 23 false positives during this period. This amounts to 97.4% recall and 96.8% precision rates in detection. The accuracy of tracking is defined as the ratio of the number of completely correct tracks and the number of correct detections. We found that 96.7% of these objects were tracked accurately over the complete period of their presence in the field of view. Similarly, the classification accuracy was measured as the ratio of the number of correct classifications and the number of correct detections, and was found to be 88%. The performance of each module is graphically depicted in Figure 6.2 . The performance of the system under different scenarios justify our claims that the system is robust to the changes in environmental conditions.

Most of the errors in object detection were caused due to inter-object occlusion or similarity of the object's color with the background. The tracking errors were caused due to multiple people with similarly colored clothes walking close to each other. In such cases our statistical models of object appearance and location were not able to distinguish between the different objects. Note

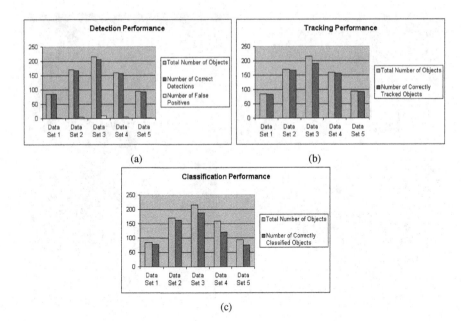

Fig. 6.2 Performance Plots. (a) Detection Performance (b) Tracking Performance. (c) Classification Performance.

that even if the objects were assigned incorrect labels due to tracking error, the trespass warning was still correctly generated if these objects were detected successfully in the danger zone by the background subtraction module. We also tested the performance of the proposed intrusion detection algorithm. This was done by first defining a danger-zone in the image (shown as yellow bounding box in Figure 6.1) and by letting the system run over a period of 7 days (day-time only). Figure 6.1 shows two different testing sites in Central Florida, along with persons, vehicles and a train detected by the system. A black bounding box around an object signifies that the object is in the danger zone. The danger zone is marked by a yellow polygon. Overall, the system detected a number of trespassing violations over its running period. When compared to the ground truth (obtained manually by browsing through the archived videos), the system was found to produce no errors during this extended period of time.

The Knight system is also being used in a number of other surveillance related projects. Recently, Knight was augmented to help the Orlando Police department with automated surveillance and was installed at four locations in the downtown Orlando area. The system was designed to provide automatic notification to a monitoring officer in case of unusual activities , such as a person falling, one or more people running, and abandoned objects. Figure 6.3 shows the cameras at the Orlando Downtown and fields of view of all four of the cameras.

The capabilities of Knight were enhanced with a correlation based ATR (Automatic Target Recognition) algorithm for robust classification of targets for a project funded by Lockheed Martin Corporation [79]. In addition, Knight is also the workhorse for a joint project with Perceptek Inc. on nighttime surveillance (using IR cameras), funded by DARPA.

Fig. 6.3 The first row shows the installed cameras at the Orlando Downtown. The second row shows the fields of view of all four cameras. The objects that are being detected, tracked and classified are shown in bounding boxes.

6.4 Conclusion

In this chapter, we present a case-study of a real-world surveillance system Knight. The system is able to detect and classify targets and seamlessly track them across multiple cameras. It also generates a summary in terms of key frames, and textual description of object trajectories and activities to a monitoring officer for final analysis and response decision. This level of interpretation was the goal of our research effort, and we believe that it is a significant step forward in the development of intelligent systems that can deal with the complexities of real world scenarios. We demonstrated the robustness of the system by extensive performance evaluation and deployment of the system in real world scenarios. Further results and information on KNIGHT can be found at $http://www.cs.ucf.edu/\sim vision/projects/Knight/Knight.html$.

Chapter 7
CONCLUDING REMARKS

7.1 What's Next?

In this book, we have identified the common problems encountered by automated video interpretation algorithms when used in realistic scenes. We have also presented solutions to many of these problems, and showed that robust object detection and classification, tracking in a single camera, and also across multiple cameras in urban areas is possible. In the future, there are two potentially important issues that still need to tackled to increase the applicability of automated surveillance systems for end users. These are discussed below.

7.1.1 Tracking Crowds

Outdoor surveillance systems frequently encounter crowds. The environments where crowd exist include airports, cinemas, railway and bus stations . Safety is an important concern in all of these areas. Thus there is a need for automated surveillance systems to have the capability of dealing with crowds. Contemporary tracking and classification methods cannot cope with crowded situations due to excessive person to person occlusion. Thus a tracker must have the ability to detect the number and position of even semi-occluded people in a scene. Some recent algorithms have started to attack subsets of the complete person location problem, by locating faces [129, 76], and determining body shape [131, 85]. One limitation of these algorithms is the requirement, that the observed person be close to the the camera or alternatively, availability of high resolution imagery. Moreover, these algorithms are computationally expensive. In our opinion, detailed person models, and the ability to recognize [60] individual body parts, e.g., hands, heads, e.t.c., is required to handle this problem. More over segmentation procedures that can distinguish between regions at different depths might also be useful. With the continued improvement in the performance of computer processors, it might be possible to combine all these cues for real time human detection and tracking in crowds, in the near future.

O. Javed, M. Shah, *Automated Multi-Camera Surveillance: Algorithms and Practice*, DOI: 10.1007/978-0-387-78881-4_7, © Springer Science+Business Media, LLC 2008

7.1.2 *Understanding Complex Human Interaction & Activities*

For any surveillance system, it will be useful to understand and predict the complex human activities taking place in the area under observation . For examples, is a group of people just walking near each other, or is the group walking *together* and interacting with each other? Is a vehicle being chased by another? is the person shop lifting in a supermarket? is a person depositing a dangerous object? This level of understanding requires knowledge at a much finer level compared to the requirements for simple detection and tracking tasks. For example, knowledge about person's facial features needs to be acquired, in order to answer questions like, is a person talking, smiling or is tense. Moreover, information about the motion of person's body parts, i.e., movement of hands and feet, and any carried objects is also required. The resolution of imagery needs to be very high to even attempt to acquire such detailed information. In addition, simple Gaussian models of humans and objects are inadequate to deal with this level of detail. Though some progress has been made with complex interaction modeling algorithms [89, 11], however, these algorithms only work in well controlled environments putting limitations on the number and location of people in the environment. Thus these algorithms are not ready for use in realistic scenarios. In our opinion, an attempt to model the 'unusual' behavior instead of detailed models of all kinds of complex human interaction might pay better dividends in context of surveillance tasks. The modeling of unusual behavior is easier since it tries to measure deviation from a single model of observed phenomenon, e.g., modeling the usual paths of object movements in a scene and trying to determine if a new object deviates from the usual paths or not [63]. One requirement for modeling of unusual behavior is the availability of long term surveillance data. We believe that the currently deployed surveillance systems can be of great help in gathering data for the development of next generation surveillance systems.

7.2 The Properties of a *Good* Surveillance System and How Knight Measures Up

A 'good' multi-camera surveillance system must be reliable. It should be easily configurable and useable. It should also be able to tune its parameters for any given scenario for better performance. An evaluation of our system according to these criteria is summarized below.

- Reliability: A reliable system must behave as expected and should have a minimum downtime . The performance of the system should also degrade gracefully under increasing load. The Knight system has been running continuously for months in downtown Orlando and was also run for extended periods of time at FDOT sites. The performance of the system in low density of people was good, and events such as entries into the danger zone were detected accurately.
- Usability: A surveillance system must be user friendly. Unlike other multi-camera tracking systems ([19, 101, 75]), our system does not need camera calibration. Note that, maintaining complete calibration of a large network of sensors is a significant maintenance task, since cameras can accidentally be moved. Our system just requires a short training phase to determine the multi-camera topology, during which the only requirement is that people move in front of the camera along the usual paths. Similarly, training for interest region detection is carried out online in an automated manner, resulting in an easy to use and robust system.
- Scalability: Increasing the number of cameras in the multi-camera surveillance system should not affect the performance of the system . Knight uses a client-server architecture, where the most computationally intensive calculations are carried out at the client side. Thus adding more cameras does not slow down the processing frame rate. Knight was tested with two and three camera setups. The drop in processing frame rate by moving from two to three cameras was negligible.

- Learning Ability: The learning ability is very important in any wide area surveillance system because the conditions in an area under observation are usually changing over time. The illumination changes with time of day. Trees and vegetation start fluttering about in windy weather. Also, in case the camera view is changed and the object classification module's performance is static, then it would not able to deal with previously unseen poses of objects for classification. In our proposed system, an unsupervised method is used for interest region detection. Moreover, the proposed interest region algorithm is adaptive,i.e, it can automatically update its parameters with changing illumination and scene conditions. The proposed object classification system also continues to update its parameters by co-training. The advantage of this approach is that the classifier is attuned to the characteristics of a particular scene. Our multi-camera tracking system requires some manual supervision during its training phase for each camera setup, but we have demonstrated that only a small number of samples are required for robust performance.

To conclude, we have presented novel video scene interpretation algorithms for solving elementary problems of automated surveillance, i.e., detection, categorization, and tracking of objects in single and multiple cameras. We have combined these algorithms in a real time system and have used it in realistic scenarios for surveillance. We believe that it is a significant step forward in the development of fully automated and intelligent video understanding systems that can deal with complexities of real world scenarios.

References

1. ACLU calls on law enforcement to support privacy laws for public video surveillance', ACLU. 08 April1999. http://www.aclu.org/news/1999/n040899b.html.
2. http://www.surveillance-and-society.org/index.htm.
3. http://safetydata.fra.dot.gov/officeofsafety/.
4. J. K. Aggarwal and Q. Cai. "Human motion analysis: A review". *Computer Vision and Image Understanding*, 73(3):428–440, 1999.
5. Orkun Alatas, Omar Javed, and Mubarak Shah. " Compressed spatio-temporal descriptors for video matching and retrieval". In *International Conference on Pattern Recognition*, 2004.
6. M. Balcan, A. Blum, and K. Yang. "Co-training and expansion: Towards briding theory and practice". In *Eighteenth Annual Conference on Neural Information Processing Systems*, 2004.
7. Y. Bar-Shalom and T.E. Foreman. *Tracking and Data Association*. Academic Press Inc., 1988.
8. S. Besson, M. Barlaud, and G. Aubert. Detection and tracking of moving objects using a level set based method. In *International Conference on Pattern Recognition*, volume 3, pages 1100–1105, 2000.
9. A. Blake and M. Isard. *Active contours*. Springer-Verlag, 1997.
10. A. Blum and T. Mitchell. "Combining labeled and unlabeled data with co-training". In *11th Annual Conference on Computational Learning Theory*, 1998.
11. A. Bobick and J. Davis. The representation and recognition of action using temporal templates. *IEEE Transactions on Pattern Analysis and Machine Intelligence*, 23(3):257–267, 2001.
12. The Defense Advanced Research Projects Agency (DARPA) Information Exploitation Office broad agency announcement. "Combat zones that see". *http://dtsn.darpa.mil/ixo/solicitations/CTS/*.
13. Q. Cai and J.K. Aggarwal. "Tracking human motion in structured environments using a distributed camera system". *IEEE Transactions on Pattern Analysis and Machine Intelligence*, 2(11):1241–1247, 1999.
14. G. Casella and R. Berger. *Statistical Inference*. Duxbury, 2 edition, 2001.
15. T.J. Cham and J. M. Rehg. A multiple hypothesis approach to figure tracking. In *IEEE International Conference on Computer Vision and Pattern Recognition*, pages 239–245, 1999.
16. D. Chetverikov and J. Verestoy. "Feature point tracking for incomplete trajectories". *Computing*, 62, Jan 1999.
17. I. Cohen, F. G. Cozman, N. Sebe, M. C. Cirelo, and T.S. Huang. "Semi-supervised learning of classifiers: Theory, algorithms for bayesian network classifiers and application to human-computer interaction.". *IEEE Transactions on Pattern Analysis and Machine Intelligence*, 26(12):1553–1567, 2004.
18. M. Collins and Y. Singer. "Unsupervised models for named entity classification". In *"Empirical Methods in Natural Language Processing"*, 99.
19. R.T. Collins, A.J. Lipton, H. Fujiyoshi, and T. Kanade. "Algorithms for cooperative multi-sensor surveillance". *Proceedings of IEEE*, 89(10):1456–1477, 2001.
20. D. Comaniciu, V. Ramesh, and P. Meer. Real-time tracking of non-rigid objects using mean shift. In *International Conference on Computer Vision and Pattern Recognition*, volume 2, pages 142–149, 2000.

21. D. Comaniciu, v. Ramesh, and P. Meer. "Kernel-based object tracking". *IEEE Transactions on Pattern Analysis and Machine Intelligence*, 25:564–575, 2003.

22. I.J. Cox and S.L. Hingorani. An efficient implementation of reid's multiple hypothesis tracking algorithm and its evaluation for the purpose of visual tracking. *IEEE Transactions on Pattern Analysis and Machine Intelligence*, 18(2):138–150, 1996.

23. R. Cutler and L. S. Davis. "Robust real-time periodic motion detection, analysis". *IEEE Transactions on Pattern Analysis and Machine Intelligence*, 22(8):809–830, Aug 2000.

24. A. P. Dempster, N. M. Laird, and D. B. Rubin. "Maximum likelihood from incomplete data via the em algorithm". *J. R. Statist. Soc. B*, 1977.

25. J. Deutscher, A. Blake, and I. Reid. Articulated body motion captured by annealed particle filtering. In *International Conference on Computer Vision and Pattern Recognition*, 2000.

26. S. L. Dockstader and A. M. Tekalp. "Multiple camera fusion for multi-object tracking". In *IEEE Workshop on Multi-Object Tracking*, 2001.

27. R. Duda, P. Hart, and D. Stork. *"Pattern classification and scene analysis"*. Wiley, 2000.

28. Yakov Bar-Shalom Ed. *MultiTarget-MultiSensor Tracking:Advanced Applications*. 1990, Artech House.

29. Editors, M. Shah, and R. Jain. *"Motion based Recognition"*. Kluwer Academic Publishers, 1990.

30. A. A. Efros, A. C. Berg, G. Mori, and J. Malik. "Recognizing action at a distance". In *iccv*, 2003.

31. A. Elgammal, R. Duraiswami, D. Harwood, and L. Davis. Background and foreground modeling using nonparametric kernel density estimation for visual surveillance. 90(7), 2002.

32. H. Farid. " Blind inverse gamma correction". *IEEE Trans. on Image Processing*, 10(10):1428–1433, Oct 2001.

33. M. Foucault. *"The Foucault Reader: An Introduction to Foucault's Thought"*. Ed. P. Rabinow, Penguin, 1991.

34. Y. Freund and R. Schapire. "Experiments with a new boosting algorithm". In *International Conference on Machine Learning*, 1996.

35. X. Gao, T.E. Boult, F. Coetzee, and V. Ramesh. Error analysis of background subtraction. In *International Conference on Computer Vision*, 2000.

36. D. M. Gavrila. The visual analysis of human movement: A survey. *Computer Vision and Image Understanding*, 73(1):82–98, 1999.

37. G. Gordon, T. Darrell, M. Harville, and J. Woodfill. Background estimation and removal based on range and color. In *International Conference on Computer Vision and Pattern Recognition*, 1999.

38. M. Greiffenhagen, V. Ramesh, and H. Nieman. " The systematic design and analysis of a vision system: A case study in video surveillance". In *Proceedings of International Conference on Computer Vision and Pattern Recognition*, 2001.

39. M. D. Grossberg and S. K. Nayar. "Determining the camera response from images: What is knowable?". *IEEE Transactions on Pattern Analysis and Machine Intelligence*, 25(11):1455–1467, November 2003.

40. M. D. Grossberg and S. K. Nayar. "Modeling the space of camera response functions". *IEEE Transactions on Pattern Analysis and Machine Intelligence*, 26(10):1272–1282, October 2004.

41. I. Haritaoglu, D. Harwood, and L.S. Davis. W4: real-time surveillance of people and their activities. *IEEE Transactions on Pattern Analysis and Machine Intelligence*, 22(8):809–830, 2000.

42. Michael Harville. " A framework for high-level feedback to adaptive per-pixel mixture of gaussian models". In *Proceedings of European Conference on Computer Vision*, 2002.

43. VSAM home page. "Visual surveillance and monitoring". *http://www-2.cs.cmu.edu/ vsam/*.

44. J. Hopcroft and R. Karp. "An $n^{2.5}$ algorithm for maximum matchings in bipartite graphs". *SIAM J. Computing*, Dec 1973.

45. B.K.P. Horn. *"Robot Vision"*. MIT Press, Cambridge, MA 1986.

46. T. Horprasert, D. Harwood, and L.S. Davis. A statistical approach for real-time robust background subtraction and shadow. In *IEEE Frame-Rate Workshop*, 1999.

47. T. Huang and S. Russell. "Object identification in a bayesian context". In *Proceedings of IJCAI,*, 1997.

48. Y. Ivanov, A. Bobick, and J. Liu. Fast lighting independent background subtraction. *International Journal of Computer Vision*, 37(2):199–207, 2000.

49. S. Jabri, Z. Duric, H. Wechsler, and A. Rosenfeld. " Detection and location of people using adaptive fusion of color and edge information". In *Proceedings of International Conference on Pattern Recognition*, 2000.

50. R. Jain, D. Militzer, and H. Nagel. "Separating non-stationary from stationary scene components in a sequence of real world tv-images". *IJCAI*, pages 612–618, 1977.

51. R. Jain and K. Wakimoto. "Multiple perspective interactive video ". In *IEEE International Conference on Multimedia Computing and Systems*, 1995.

52. O. Javed and M. Shah. "Tracking and object classification for automated surveillance". In *European Conference on Computer Vision*, volume 4, pages 343–357, 2002.

53. Omar Javed, Saad Ali, and Mubarak Shah. "Online detection and classification of moving objects using progressively improving detectors". In *International Conference on Computer Vision and Pattern Recognition*, 2005.

54. Omar Javed, Sohaib Khan, Zeeshan Rasheed, and Mubarak Shah. "Visual content based segmentation of talk and game shows". *International Journal of Computers and Applications*, June 2002.

55. Omar Javed, Zeeshan Rasheed, Orkun Alatas, Asad Hakeem, and Mubarak Shah. "Real time surveillance in multiple non-overlapping cameras". In *Demonstration in CVPR*, 2003.

56. Omar Javed, Zeeshan Rasheed, Orkun Alatas, and Mubarak Shah. "Knight-m: A real time surveillance system for multiple overlapping and non-overlapping cameras". In *IEEE Proc. of ICME*, 2003.

57. Omar Javed, Zeeshan Rasheed, Khurram Shafique, and Mubarak Shah. Tracking across multiple cameras with disjoint views. In *International Conference on Computer Vision*, 2003.

58. Omar Javed, Khurram Shafique, and Mubarak Shah. "A hierarchical approach to robust background subtraction using color and gradient information". In *Workshop on Motion and Video Computing*, pages 22–27, 2002.

59. Omar Javed, Khurram Shafique, and Mubarak Shah. "Appearance modeling for tracking in multiple non-overlapping cameras". In *International Conference on Computer Vision and Pattern Recognition*, 2005.

60. Omar Javed, Mubarak Shah, and Dorin Comaniciu. " A probabilitic framework for object recognition in video". In *International Conference on Image Processing*, 2004.

61. A. D. Jepson, D. J. Fleet, and T. F. El-Maraghi. Robust online appearance models for visual tracking. *IEEE Transactions on Pattern Analysis and Machine Intelligence*, 25(10):1296–1311, 2003.

62. T. Joachims. "Transductive inference for text classification using support vector machines". In *16th International Conference on Machine Learning*, 1999.

63. Imran Junejo, Omar Javed, and Mubarak Shah. " Multi feature path modeling for video surveillance". In *International Conference on Pattern Recognition*, 2004.

64. J. Kang, I. Cohen, and G. Medioni. "Continuous tracking within and across camera streams". In *International Conference on Computer Vision and Pattern Recognition*, 2003.

65. M. Kass, A. Witkin, and D. Terzopoulos. " Bayesian multi-camera surveillance". In *International Conference on Computer Vision*, 1987.

66. V. Kettnaker and R. Zabih. "Bayesian multi-camera surveillance". In *International Conference on Computer Vision and Pattern Recognition*, pages 117–123, 1999.

67. S. Khan and M. Shah. "Tracking people in presence of occlusion". In *Asian Conference on Computer Vision*, 2000.

68. S. Khan and M. Shah. "Consistent labeling of tracked objects in multiple cameras with overlapping fields of view". *IEEE Transactions on Pattern Analysis and Machine Intelligence*, 25, 2003.

69. D. Koller, J. Webber, T. Huang, J. Malik, G. Ogasawara, B. Rao, and S. Russel. " Towards robust automatic traffic scene analysis in real time ". In *Proceedings of International Conference on Pattern Recognition*, 1994.

70. C. G. Lambert, S. E. Harrington, C. R. Harvey, and A. Glodjo. "Efficient on-line nonparametric kernal density estimation". *Algorithmica*, 25, 1999.

71. L. Lee, R. Romano, and G. Stein. "Monitoring activities from multiple video streams: Establishing a common coordinate frame". *IEEE Trans. on Pattern Recognition and Machine Intelligence*, 22(8):758–768, Aug 2000.

72. K. Levi and Y. Weiss. "Learning object detection from a small number of examples: The importance of good features". In *International Conference on Computer Vision and Pattern Recognition*, 2004.

73. A. Levin, P. Viola, and Y. Freund. "Unsupervised improvement of visual detectors using co-training". In *International Conference on Computer Vision*, 2003.

74. Q. Li and J. Racine. "Nonparameteric estimation of distributions with categorical and continuous data". *Journal of Multivariate Analysis*, 86:266–292, 2003.

75. Ser-Nam Lim, Larry S. Davis, and Ahmed Elgammal. " A scalable image-based multicamera visual surveillance system". In *IEE Conference on Advanced Video and Signal Based Surveillance*, 2003.

76. Z. Liu and Y. Wang. "Face detection and tracking in video using dynamic programming". In *IEEE International Conference on Image Processing*, 2000.

77. L. Liyuan and L. Maylor. Integrating intensity and texture differences for robust change detection. *IEEE Trans. on Image Processing*, 11(2):105–112, 2002.

78. Bruce D. Lucas and Takeo Kanade. An iterative image registration technique with an application to stereo vision. In *International Joint Conference on Artificial Intelligence*, 1981.

79. A. Mahalanobis, J. Cannon, S. R. Stanfill, R. Muise, and M. Shah. "Network video image processing for security, surveillance, and situational awareness". In *SPIE Defense and Security Symposium*, 2004.

80. D. Makris, T. J. Ellis, and J. K. Black. "Bridging the gaps between cameras ". In *International Conference on Computer Vision and Pattern Recognition*, 2004.

81. S. Mann and R. Picard. "Being undigital with digital cameras: Extending dynamic range by combining differently exposed pictures". In *Proc. IS&T 46th Annual Conference*, 1995.

82. T. Matsuyama, T. Ohya, , and H. Habe. " Background subtraction for nonstationary scenes". In *Proceedings of Asian Conference on Computer Vision*, 2000.

83. S. J. McKenna, S. Jabri, Z. Duric, H. Wechsler, and A. Rosenfeld. Tracking groups of people. *Computer Vision and Image Understanding*, 2000.

84. A. Mittal and L.S. Davis. "M2 tracker: a multi-view approach to segmenting and tracking people in a cluttered scene". *International Journal of Computer Vision*, 51(3):189–203, 2003.

85. T.B. Moeslund and E. Granum. A survey of computer vision-based human motion capture. *Computer Vision and Image Understanding*, 2001.

86. A. Monnet, A. Mittal, N. Paragios, and V. Ramesh. Background modeling and subtraction of dynamic scenes. In *International Conference on Computer Vision*, 2003.

87. K. Nigam, A. McCallum, S. Thrun, and T. Mitchell. "Text classification from labeled and unlabeled documents using EM". *Maching Learning*, 30(2-3):103–134, 2000.

88. N. Ohta. "A statistical approach to background subtraction for surveillance systems ". In *International Conference on Computer Vision*, 2001.

89. N.M. Oliver, B. Rosario, and A. Pentland. A bayesian computer vision system for modeling human interactions. *IEEE Transactions on Pattern Analysis and Machine Intelligence*, 22(8):831–843, 2000.

90. T. J. Olson and F. Z. Brill. "Moving object detection and event recognition algorithm for smart cameras". In *Proceedings of 1997 Image Understanding Workshop*, pages 159–175, 1997.

91. M. Oren and S. K. Nayar. "Generalization of the lambertian model and implications for machine vision". *International Journal of Computer Vision*, 14(3):227–251, April 1995.

92. G. Orwell. *"1984"*. Signet Book, 1949.

93. N. Oza. "Online ensemble learning". In *Ph.D. dissertation*, 2002.

94. C. Papageorgiou and T. Poggio. "Trainable pedestrian detections". In *International Conference on Image Processing*, 1999.

95. N. Paragios and R. Deriche. Geodesic active contours and level sets for the detection and tracking of moving objects. *IEEE Transactions on Pattern Analysis and Machine Intelligence*, 22(3):266–280, 2000.

96. D. Pierce and C. Cardie. "Limitations of co-training for natural language learning from large datasets". In *Conference on Empirical Methods in Natural Language Processing*, 2001.

97. R. Polana and R. Nelson. "Detection and recognition of periodic, non-rigid motion". *International Journal of Computer Vision*, 23(3):261–282', 1997.

98. F. Porikli. "Inter-camera color calibration using cross-correlation model function". In *International Conference on Image Processing*, 2003.

99. A. Rahimi and T. Darrell. "Simultaneous calibration and tracking with a network of non-overlapping sensors". In *International Conference on Computer Vision and Pattern Recognition*, 2004.

100. K. Rangarajan and M. Shah. Establishing motion correspondence. *Computer Vision, Graphics and Image Processing*, 54(1):56–73, 1991.

101. C. Regazzoni, V. Ramesh, and G. Foresti. "Scanning the issue/technology: Special issue on video communications, processing and understanding for third generation surveillance systems". *Proceedings of the IEEE*, 89(10):1355–1366, October 2001.

102. Y. Ricquebourg and P. Bouthemy. "Real time tracking of moving persons by exploiting spatiotemporal image slices ". *IEEE Transactions on Pattern Analysis and Machine Intelligence*, 22(8), Aug 2000.

103. J. Rittscher, J. Kato, S. Joga, and A. Blake. A probabilistic background model for tracking. In *European Conference on Computer Vision*, volume 2, pages 336–350, 2000.

104. K. Rohr. Toward model-based recognition of human movements in imagesequences. *Computer Vision, Graphics and Image Processing*, 59, 1994.

105. M Yeddanapudi S. De, K. R. Pattipati, and Y. Bar-Shalom. "A generalized s-d assignment algorithm for multi-sensor multi-target state estimation ". *IEEE Trans. on Aerospace and Electronic Systems*, 33(2), 1997.

106. H. Schneiderman and T. Kanade. "A statistical method for 3d object detection applied to faces and cars". In *International Conference on Computer Vision and Pattern Recognition*, 2000.

107. S.M. Seitz and C.R. Dyer. View-invariant analysis of cyclic motion. *International Journal of Computer Vision*, 25:1–25, 1997.

108. I.K. Sethi and R. Jain. Finding trajectories of feature points in a monocular image sequence. *IEEE Transactions on Pattern Analysis and Machine Intelligence*, 9(1):56–73, 1987.

109. J.A. Sethian. *Level set methods: evolving interfaces in geometry,fluid mechanics computer vision and material sciences*. Cambridge University Press, 1996.

110. K. Shafique and M. Shah. "A non-iterative greedy algorithm for multi-frame point correspondence". In *International Conference on Computer Vision*, 2003.

111. Y. Shan and H. S. Sahwney amd R. Kumar. "Unsupervised learning of discriminative edge measures for vehicle matching between non-overlapping cameras". In *International Conference on Computer Vision and Pattern Recognition*, 2005.

112. D. Shen, J. Zhang, J. Su, G. Zhou, and C. L. Tan. "A collaborative ability measurement for co-training". In *International Joint Conference on Natural Language Processing*, 2004.

113. Mubarak Shah Sohaib Khan, Omar Javed. " Tracking in uncalibrated cameras with overlapping field of view". In *Performance Evaluation of Tracking and Surveillance PETS (with IEEE CVPR)*, 2001.

114. C. Stauffer. "Learning to track objects through un-observed regions". In *Proceedings of IEEE Workshop on Motion*, 2005.

115. C. Stauffer and W.E.L. Grimson. Learning patterns of activity using real time tracking. *IEEE Transactions on Pattern Analysis and Machine Intelligence*, 22(8):747–767, 2000.

116. Bjoern Stenger, Visvanathan Ramesh, Nikos Paragios, Frans Coetzee, and Joachim M. Buhmann. Topology free hidden markov models: Application to background modeling. In *International Conference on Computer Vision*, 2001.

117. M. J. Swain and D. H. Ballard. "Indexing via color histograms". In *International Conference on Computer Vision*, 1990.

118. Nick Taylor. "State surveillance and right to privacy". *Surveillance and Society*, 1(1):66–86, 2002.

119. Ting-Hsun, Chang, and Shaogang Gong. "Tracking multiple people with a multi-camera system". In *IEEE Workshop on Multi-Object Tracking*, 2001.

120. M. E. Tipping and C. M. Bishop. "Probabilistic principal component analysis". *Journal of the Royal Statistical Society, Series B*, 61(3):611–622, 1999.

121. K. Toyama, B. Brumitt J. Krumm, and B. Meyers. "Wallflower: Principles and practices of background".

122. Ping-Sing Tsai, Mubarak Shah, Katharine Keiter, and Takis Kasparis. "Cyclic motion detection for motion based recognition". *Pattern Recognition*, 1994.

123. C.J. Veenman, M.J. Reinders, and E. Backer. Resolving motion correspondence for densely moving points. *IEEE Transactions on Pattern Analysis and Machine Intelligence*, 23(1):54–72, 2001.

124. P. Viola and M. Jones. "Robust real time face detectio". *International Journal of Computer Vision*, 56(1):17–36, 2004.

125. P. Viola, M. Jones, and D. Snow. "Detecting pedestrians using patterns of motion and appearance". In *International Conference on Computer Vision*, 2003.

126. M.P. Wand and M.C. Jones. *Kernel Smoothing*. Chapman & Hall, 1994.

127. D. Williams and M. Shah. "A fast algorithm for active contours and curvature estimation". *Computer Vision, Graphics and Image Processing*, 55(1):14–26, 1992.

128. C.R. Wren, A. Azarbayejani, and A. Pentland. "Pfinder: Real-time tracking of the human body". *IEEE Transactions on Pattern Analysis and Machine Intelligence*, 19(7):780–785, 1997.

129. Ming-Hsuan Yang, D. J. Kriegman, and N. Ahuja. "Detecting faces in images: a survey". *IEEE Transactions on Pattern Analysis and Machine Intelligence*, 24(1), 2002.

130. D. Zhang, S. Z. Li, and D. Perez. "Real-time face detection using boosting in hierarchical feature spaces". In *International Conference on Pattern Recognition*, 2004.

131. T. Zhao and R. Nevatia. "Stochastic human segmentation from a static camera". In *IEEE Workshop on Motion and Video Computing*, 2000.

132. T. Zhao, R. Nevatia, and F. Lv. "Segmentation and tracking of multiple humans in complex situation". In *International Conference on Computer Vision and Pattern Recognition*, 2001.

133. J. Zhong and S. Sclaroff. Segmenting foreground objects from a dynamic textured background via a robust kalman filter. In *International Conference on Computer Vision*, 2003.

Index